POLITICS AND RELIGION

D1416979

CAC Publishing
Center for Action and Contemplation
cac.org

"*Oneing*" is an old English word that was used by Lady Julian of Norwich (1342–1416) to describe the encounter between God and the soul. The Center for Action and Contemplation proudly borrows the word to express the divine unity that stands behind all of the divisions, dichotomies, and dualisms in the world. We pray and publish with Jesus' words, "that all may be one" (John 17:21).

EDITOR:
Vanessa Guerin

ASSOCIATE EDITOR:
Shirin McArthur

PUBLISHER:
The Center for Action and Contemplation

ADVISORY BOARD:
David Benner
James Danaher
Ilia Delio, OSF
Sheryl Fullerton
Stephen Gaertner, OPraem
Ruth Patterson

Design and Composition by Nelson Kane Design

Oneing

VOLUME 5 NO. 2

EDITOR'S NOTE

Not to speak, is to speak. Not to act, is to act.
—Dietrich Bonhoeffer

WHEN THE THEME of this edition of *Oneing* was first considered, my initial thoughts were of my childhood in Latin America. My father was a Foreign Service officer with the US Agency for International Development and it was taboo to discuss politics and religion in any social context whatsoever. It wasn't until I returned to the US and settled in Washington, DC, during the Viet Nam War, that I realized how sheltered my life had been.

Peace marches and protests were my rites of initiation and, as I look back, even my art work was an abstract reflection of what I was experiencing at the time. Although I managed to escape being dragged off to jail, the memories of certain friends and their experiences were reawakened when I read Peter Armstrong's article, "Faith in a Prison Cell." Peter recounts in detail the hours leading up to his act of civil disobedience, protesting the death penalty on the steps of the US Supreme Court. His arrest and subsequent sixteen hours in the Washington, DC Jail, while harrowing, were transformative for him.

Rev. angel Kyodo williams endured a long, fascinating journey through a chaotic childhood, including an experience of Christianity "by way of the Black Baptist Church [she] was made to go to...by an abusive babysitter-turned-pseudo-mom." By the time she was in high school, she had abandoned Christianity altogether and began to explore a newfound independence. Through embracing engagement with many challenging opportunities as a young, black, gay woman, she ultimately discovered her authentic self, "landed...on a [meditation] cushion" in a Buddhist temple, and found a spiritual home. From this fresh perspective, she has been able to "bridge the worlds of transformation and justice."

Contemplative practice grounds Catholic Sister Simone Campbell, an attorney and activist, in her work for social justice "at the intersection of politics and religion." Globally recognized for her lobbying ministry as the leader of NETWORK, a Catholic social justice organization, her rootedness in gospel values gives her the impetus to "lobby on Capitol Hill on issues of income and wealth disparity in our nation." As she puts it, "God is alive in all.... No one can be left out of my care."

"More wars have been waged, and are being waged, in the name of religion than we would like to acknowledge," writes poet and peace activist Avideh Shashaani in her article, "Stone and Star." "If we take the three Abrahamic religions—Judaism, Christianity, and Islam—that have the same patriarch and are all monotheistic religions, should we not ask ourselves why they are fighting with such fervor?"

Islamic scholar John Esposito enlightens us with a well-developed history of modern Middle Eastern politics and religion, which helps us understand the rise of "a significant and dangerous minority of extremists, *jihad* groups from Egypt to Indonesia, al-Qaeda and ISIS," and their "theology of hate." Unfortunately, "most experts and citizens in Muslim countries do not expect significant reform any time soon," even though "the call for greater political participation and democratization has become widespread in many countries in the Muslim world."

At this point in history, with the current state of political and religious events shifting daily, this edition of *Oneing* is an especially critical one. I encourage you to read each article with your eyes—and ears—wide open. Many of the contributors fearlessly speak truth to power; as Richard Rohr states in his Introduction, "There is no such thing as being non-political. Everything we say or do either affirms or critiques the status quo. Even *to say nothing is to say something*."

Vanessa Guerin,
Editor

CONTRIBUTORS

RICHARD ROHR, OFM, is a Franciscan priest of the New Mexico Province and the Founding Director of the Center for Action and Contemplation in Albuquerque, New Mexico. An internationally recognized author and spiritual leader, Fr. Richard teaches primarily on incarnational mysticism, non-dual consciousness, and contemplation, with a particular emphasis on how these affect the social justice issues of our time. Along with many recorded conferences, he is the author of numerous books, including *The Divine Dance: The Trinity and Your Transformation* (with Mike Morrell) and *A Spring Within Us: A Book of Daily Meditations*. To learn more about Fr. Richard Rohr and the CAC, visit https://cac.org/richard-rohr/richard-rohr-ofm/.

THE REV. WESLEY GRANBERG-MICHAELSON has served as chief legislative assistant to Senator Mark O. Hatfield, as Associate Editor of *Sojourners* magazine, as Director of Church and Society for the World Council of Churches, and as General Secretary of the Reformed Church in America. The author of six previous books, his forthcoming *Future Faith* will explore the ten major challenges posed by changes in world Christianity and their impact on US congregations. To learn more about Wes Granberg-Michaelson, visit https://eerdword.com/2011/06/29/the-story-of-wesley-granberg-michaelson-by-jon-pott/.

THE REV. RACHEL M. SRUBAS is the author of *The Girl Got Up: A Cruciform Memoir*, *City of Prayer: Forty Days with Desert Christians*, and *Oblation: Meditations on St. Benedict's Rule*. Her essays and poems have appeared in *The Best American Poetry*, *The Christian Century*, *America*, and numerous other periodicals. She is a Minister of Word and Sacrament in the Presbyterian Church (USA) and an oblate (non-monastic affiliate) of the Order of St. Benedict. Rachel is also a spiritual director who teaches on the faculty of the Hesychia School of Spiritual Direction in Tucson, Arizona, where she lives with her husband, Ken McAllister. To learn more about Rachel Srubas, visit http://www.tucsonspiritualdirection.org.

JOAN D. CHITTISTER, OSB, a Benedictine Sister of Erie, Pennsylvania, is one of the most influential religious and social leaders of our time. For forty years, Joan has passionately advocated on behalf of peace, human rights, women's issues, and church renewal. Executive director of Benetvision, she is a sought-after speaker, counselor, and clear voice that bridges all religions. Joan is also a best-selling author of more than fifty books, including her most recent, *Radical Spirit: 12 Ways to Live a Free and Authentic Life*. She has written hundreds of articles, an online column for the *National Catholic Reporter*, and a blog for The *Huffington Post*. To learn more about Joan Chittister, visit http://www.joanchittister.org/.

LEE STAMAN, MLIS, is the Systems Librarian at the Center for Action and Contemplation. Currently his work is focused on cataloging everything Richard Rohr has said and written. Lee has a passion for the role of information and technology in the modern world, along with a deep interest in the history of religious thought. He has degrees in philosophy and theology and resides in Seattle, Washington, with his wife and two children. He reads aloud from the Patristics to put them to sleep. Lee Staman may be contacted at lstaman@cac.org.

ROSE MARIE BERGER, a native of California, has been on the Sojourners staff since 1986. Her career has spanned over thirty years of faith-based activism, advocacy journalism, and pastoral leadership. Rose is an organizer, pastoral leader, teacher of biblical literacy, poet, and author. Her books include *Drawn By God: A History of the Society of Catholic Medical Missionaries from 1967 to 1991* (with Janet Gottschalk) and *Who Killed Donte Manning? The Story of an American Neighborhood*. Rose has lived in the Columbia Heights neighborhood of Washington, DC, since the mid-1980s. To learn more about Rose Berger, visit http://rosemarieberger.com/about/.

ZACCARY HANEY, OPRAEM, is a simply professed brother of the Norbertine Community of Santa Maria de la Vid Abbey in Albuquerque, New Mexico. Raised in Wisconsin, he lived in Chicago for two years before relocating to New Mexico and entering the abbey in 2015. Zaccary holds a BA in religious studies from St. Norbert College and a MA in religion from the University of Chicago Divinity School, where he focused his studies on medieval Christian thought. He is currently studying for his Master of Divinity at Catholic Theological Union in Chicago. Zaccary Haney may be contacted at zac.haney@outlook.com.

SIMONE CAMPBELL, SSS, has served as Executive Director of NETWORK since 2004. She is a religious leader, attorney, and poet with extensive experience in public policy and advocacy for systemic change. In Washington, DC, Sr. Simone lobbies on issues of economic justice, immigration reform, and healthcare. During the 2010 congressional debate about healthcare reform, she wrote and gathered signatures for the famous "nuns' letter" which was cited by many as critically important in passing the Affordable Care Act. In 2012, Sr. Simone was instrumental in organizing the "Nuns on the Bus" tour of nine states to oppose the "Ryan Budget." She is the author of *A Nun on the Bus: How All of Us Can Create Hope, Change, and Community*. To learn more about Sr. Simone Campbell, visit https://networklobby.org/staff/SimoneCampbellSSS/.

ERIC MARTIN is a doctoral candidate in systematic theology at Fordham University and co-editor of *The Berrigan Letters: Personal Correspondence of Daniel and Philip Berrigan*. He teaches classes on The Catholic Worker and The Bible and Social Justice, and is working on his dissertation, "A Theology of Dis/Obedience: The Conversion of Daniel Berrigan, 1953–1966." Eric Martin may be contacted at emartin31@fordham.edu.

PETER ARMSTRONG is a first-year seminarian at Yale Divinity School. Although he didn't grow up religious, Peter found his way to Christianity during his college years through a study of various world religions, personal discernment, and a practice of contemplative prayer. After graduating from Georgetown's School of Foreign Service in 2015, he explored faith and justice through two consecutive service corps programs: The Episcopal Service Corps in St. Louis, MO, and Sojourners in Washington, DC. In addition to studying at Yale Divinity School, Peter is enrolled in the Center for Action and Contemplation's Living School for Action and Contemplation. Peter Armstrong may be contacted at peter.armstrong@yale.edu or tagged @petertarmstrong.

MICHAEL PLEKON, PhD, a priest in the Orthodox Church in America, is attached to St. Gregory the Theologian Orthodox Church, Wappingers Falls, New York. Michael is Professor Emeritus in the departments of Sociology and Anthropology and Religion and Culture at Baruch College of the City University of New York. His areas of specialization include the social history of American religious traditions and communities, social theory and its connections with theology, the social and theological thought of Søren Kierkegaard, contemporary Eastern Orthodox theology and theologians of the Russian emigration, and saints, canonized or not, in our time. He is the author of numerous books, including *Saints as They Really Are, The Church Has Left the Building, The World as Sacrament*, and *Uncommon Prayer*. To learn more about Michael Plekon, visit http://www.baruch.cuny.edu/wsas/academics/anthropology/mplekon.htm.

Shirin McArthur, MDiv, is a spiritual guide, writer, poet, and editor who lives in Arizona. She is a former CAC staff member and the Associate Editor of *Oneing*. Shirin leads retreats and Embodied Prayer experiences and her contemplative photography appears daily at https://www.instagram.com/shirinmcarthur/. Shirin's award-winning Prayerful Pondering blog, part of the Christian Century network, will soon transition from https://shirinmcarthur.wordpress.com to her forthcoming website: shirinmcarthur.com. Shirin McArthur may be contacted at shirin@communicationclarified.com.

Avideh Shashaani, PhD, is founder of the Fund for the Future of our Children (FFC). Established in 1993, FFC focuses on empowering young people to be leaders for peace and justice. She is a recipient of the "Waging Peace" award instituted by former President Jimmy Carter. Avideh was the first co-director of the International Institute for Rehabilitation in Developing Countries, founded by the United Nations. She is the author of three books of poetry, including *Tell Me Where to Be Born*, which focuses on violence against children worldwide. Avideh holds a doctorate in Sufi Studies and has been a speaker in forums such as the United Nations Conference on Human Rights and Parliament of World Religions. To learn more about Avideh Shashaani, visit http://www.futureofchildren.net/ffcs-mission/avideh-shashaani-president.

John L. Esposito, PhD, is Professor of Religion and International Affairs and of Islamic Studies at Georgetown University, and Founding Director of the Prince Alwaleed Bin Talal Center for Muslim-Christian Understanding in the Walsh School of Foreign Service. Esposito has served as editor for seven of Oxford's Islamic Encyclopedias and Dictionaries and is the author of more than forty-five books and monographs, including *Islamophobia and the Challenge of Pluralism in the 21st Century*, *Unholy War: Terror in the Name of Islam*, *The Islamic Threat: Myth or Reality?* and *Women in Muslim Family Law*. His books and articles have been translated into more than thirty-five languages. To learn more about John Esposito, visit http://explore.georgetown.edu/people/jle2/.

The Rev. angel Kyodo williams, Sensei, is an author, maverick spiritual teacher, master trainer, and founder of the Center for Transformative Change. She has been bridging the worlds of personal transformation and justice since the publication of her critically acclaimed book, *Being Black: Zen and the Art of Living with Fearlessness and Grace*. Her book was hailed as "an act of love" by Pulitzer Prize-winner Alice Walker and "a classic" by Buddhist teacher Jack Kornfield. Ordained as a Zen priest, angel recently became the second black woman recognized as a teacher in her lineage. To learn more about angel Kyodo williams, visit http://angelkyodowilliams.com/.

INTRODUCTION

T HE ETYMOLOGY OF words is often a great place to start when exploring a topic or idea. *Religio* means to reconnect, which was apparently seen as God's unique work. *Polis*–which led to the word politics–simply means city or public forum or the aggregated world of people.

This gets us off to a great start. We live in a very disconnected or unconnected world, and thus are quite unreligious or irreligious–even the many who regularly attend church, synagogue, or mosque. (I know that is not the common perception today with the prevalent use of social media, but my assumption here is that this superficial "connecting" is part of the problem because it makes us think we are in contact when often we are not at all.)

One of the pieces that has historically remained the most disconnected for many religious people has been the public forum. Unlike its Jewish forebears, Christianity, in its first two thousand years, has kept its morality mostly private, personal, interior, fervent, and heavenbound, but with very few direct implications for what is now called our collective economic, social, or political life. Politics and religion remained largely in two different realms, unless religion was uniting with empires. Yes, we looked to Rome and Constantinople for imperial protection, but little did we realize the price we would eventually pay for such a compromise with foundational Gospel values.

This convenient split took the form of either the inner or the outer world. We religious folks were supposed to be the inner people while the outer world was left to politicians, scientists, and workers of every stripe. Now this is all catching up with us, as even the inner world has largely been overtaken by psychology, literature, and the huge world of self-help. Fewer and fewer people now expect religion to have anything to say about either the inner or outer worlds!

If we do not go deep and in, we cannot go far and wide.

Now, in my opinion, the reason we lost our Christian authority is because we did not talk about the inner world very well (believing doctrines, practicing rituals, and following requirements are not, in and of themselves, inner or deep). Frankly, Buddhism did the inner far better than the three monotheistic religions. We Christians did not connect the inner with the outer—which is a consequence of not going *in* deeply enough. We now have become increasingly *irrelevant*, often to the very people who want to go both deep and far. We so disconnected from the political—God's aggregated people, the public forum—that soon we had nothing much to say.

I am not talking about *partisan politics* here, but simply the connecting of the inner world with the outer world. We have allowed the word partisan to be the first and sometimes only meaning of the word political (another sad result of our dualistic thinking), and so people do not even allow us to preach the purely Gospel message from the pulpit—as it might sound "political"! Our dualistic way of thinking allowed us to be hamstrung and silenced.

Politicians on the Right normally love this, because we thereby become easy friends of the status quo and, if we dare to critique it, we will be called "political"—as if this is a terrible thing to be. If we affirm the status quo, we will be called loyal, conservative, Christian, and faith-based! It is no surprise that President Trump wants to remove the prohibition on religious groups taking political stands. He knows they will reliably be on the side of the status quo because they usually want to *conserve* the privileges of the comfortable (the clergy themselves usually being in the comfortable class). This was the very thing that St. Francis wanted to change in his community.

Here is my major point: There is no such thing as being non-political. Everything we say or do either affirms or critiques the status quo. Even *to say nothing is to say something*: The status quo—even if it is massively unjust and deceitful—is apparently okay. This "non-political" stance is an illusion and the powerful have always been able to rely upon what Vladimir Lenin (1870–1924) called "useful idiots." Many church people do not know that they are often used as useful idiots on issues like the total legitimacy of the State of Israel or the war machine, the not-so-obvious biases of the budget, the single-issue voting of many "pro-life" Christians, the willingness to call the Gospel "Socialism," and on and on.

We cannot allow Christianity to be used as useful idiocy any longer. We must use the power of the Gospel to critique and affirm both the Left and the Right of most public positions, knowing that the Left normally does not represent the Gospel either, but is also another power-and-control position. Its primary advantage is that it has developed a critical mind—but, even there, it often becomes too negative and too critical.

The Left often does not know how to both "transcend and include," which is true non-partisan and healthy politics and religion. In its idealism, it often becomes ideological, arrogant, dualistic, individualistic—problem-solver more than reconstructionist—and thus something other than Love.

Where then do we go? This does leave us with almost "nowhere to lay [our] heads" (see Luke 9:58). This is the essential powerlessness of Gospel power—or is it? The Hebrew Prophets, Jesus, Buddha, Francis, and Gandhi first appear to be "nothing," outside the system, and really of no consequence. But just wait a while. It is these wisdom figures who offer the real and final power. Like leaven and yeast, their much deeper assumptions rise, again and again, in every age, while kings, tyrants, ideologies, and empires keep changing and passing away.

Richard Rohr

From Mysticism to Politics

By Wes Granberg-Michaelson

E VERYTHING BEGINS IN mysticism and ends in politics."[1] So wrote Charles Péguy (1873–1914), a French poet and writer who lived in solidarity with workers and peasants and became deeply influenced by Catholic faith in the last years of his life.[2] This provocative quote identifies the foundational starting point for how faith and politics should relate.

Usually, however, we get it backward. Our temptation is to begin with politics and then try to figure out how religion can fit in. We start with the accepted parameters of political debate and, whether we find ourselves on the left or the right, we use religion to justify and bolster our existing commitments. Those holding political power are adept at exploiting this temptation. They see religious groups as another "demographic" which can be harnessed to advance a party's or a president's political agenda. That pattern has been evidenced most vividly in the last three decades by the unholy marriage between the "Religious Right" and the Republican Party, although, historically, this danger knew no partisan boundaries.

But what if we make the inward journey our starting point? What if we recognize that our engagement in politics should be rooted in our participation in the Trinitarian flow of God's love? Then everything changes. We are no longer guided or constrained by what we think is politically possible, but are compelled by what we know is most real. At the heart of all creation, the mutual love within the Trinity overflows to embrace all of life. We are invited to participate in the transforming power of this love. There we discover the ground of our being, centering all our life and action.

This was revealed most fully in Jesus, as God's Son. His love for enemies, his non-violent response to evil, his embrace of the marginalized, his condemnation of self-serving religious hypocrites, his compassion for the poor, his disregard for boundaries of social exclusion, his advocacy for the economically oppressed, and his certainty that God's reign was breaking into the world all flowed from his complete, mutual participation in his Father's love. Jesus didn't merely show the way; he lived completely in the presence and power of God's redeeming, transforming life.

This didn't fit any conventional political alternative in Palestine at the time. Jesus wasn't a Zealot, seeking the violent overthrow of an oppressive empire, although he welcomed a Zealot as his disciple, resisted and undermined the authority of political rulers, and was crucified as "King of the Jews." He refused to identify with religious authorities who were willing to compromise their spiritual convictions to foster their collusion with imperial political power. Yet, the "politics of Jesus" presented a clear agenda for radical social and economic transformation in his time, as in ours.[3]

All this was rooted, however, in the incarnate participation of Jesus in the love of the Trinity. His life embodied what God's love intends for the world and demonstrated the Spirit's power to transform, heal, and make whole what is broken. Further, Jesus' clarity about his identity preceded his action. Before beginning his ministry with his message of liberation found in Luke 4, Jesus wandered in the wilderness for forty days, encountering his demons, resisting false idols, relying solely on his trust in God, and emerging "filled with the power of the Spirit" (see Luke 4:14). Only then did he proclaim his mission of liberty to captives, recovery of sight to the blind, freeing of the oppressed, and proclaiming the year of God's favor (see Luke 4:18–19). His mysticism preceded and then accompanied his politics.

TRANSFORMATIVE CHANGE IN politics depends so much on having a clear view of the desired end. Where does that vision come from? Possibilities may be offered by various ideologies, or party platforms, or political candidates. But, for the person of faith, that vision finds its roots in God's intended and preferred future for the world. It comes not as a dogmatic blueprint but as an experiential encounter with God's love, flowing like a river from God's throne, nourishing trees with leaves for the healing of the nations (see Revelation 22:1–2). This biblically infused vision, resonant from Genesis to Revelation, pictures a world made whole, with people living in a beloved community, where no one is despised or forgotten, peace reigns, and the goodness of God's creation is treasured and protected as a gift.

Such a vision strikes the political pragmatist as idyllic, unrealistic, and irrelevant. But the person of faith, whose inward journey opens his or her life to the explosive love of God, knows that this vision is the most real of all. It is a glimpse of creation's purpose and a glimmering of the Spirit's movement amid the world's present pain, brokenness, and despair. This vision also recognizes the inevitable journey of inward and outward transformation—the simultaneous, continuing transformation of the inward hearts of people liberated by God's astonishing grace and the outward transformation of social and economic structures liberated by God's standards of justice.

So, for the Christian, politics entails an inevitable spiritual journey. But this is not the privatized expression of belief which keeps faith in Jesus contained in an individualized bubble and protects us from the "world." The experience of true faith in the living God is always personal and never individual. Rather, it is a spiritual journey which connects us intrinsically to the presence of God, whose love yearns to save and transform the world. We are called to be "in Christ," which means we share—always imperfectly, and always in community with others—the call to be the embodiment of God's love in the world.

I F THIS IS where politics for the person of faith begins, then where does it go and how might it end?

Mahatma Gandhi (1869–1948) once reportedly said, "The means is the end in the making," and we frequently hear the admonition to "be the change that you want to see." What we should recognize at the outset is that the methods, means, and style by which we engage in politics determines the end. In the present US political climate, this presents tremendous difficulties. Polarized, binary, either/or approaches to political participation have become hard-wired into conventional politics. The establishment of Fox News by the late Roger Ailes (1940–2017); the growth of cable news avenues with singular perspectives; the promiscuous presence of social media, allowing one to see the whole world through a biased lens; and the pressure to reduce issues to competing sound bites all contribute to a toxic political environment where participants talk at each other instead of with one another.

Overcoming this polarity becomes hard because patently clear moral issues of right and wrong seem plainly and painfully at stake. I once wrote Richard Rohr a note, which said, "Donald Trump makes it very hard for me to get beyond dualistic thinking." Maintaining moral clarity is essential, and evidenced so clearly by the biblical prophets, Jesus, and those transformative prophets who have followed: Francis of Assisi (1181–1226), Archbishop Oscar Romero (1917–1980), Dorothy Day (1897–1980), Martin Luther King, Jr. (1929–1968), and so many more. The challenges of climate change, immigration, healthcare, economic inequality, racism, and blind trust in military might are not simply political issues but profoundly moral choices. Biblical wisdom offers direct and unambiguous judgments on these and other questions which can't be compromised and must frame the perspectives of we who embrace this faith.

But starting with mysticism means we experience the gift of the intrinsic wholeness and interconnection in all of creation. Each person is held within this web of gracious love. Thus, we begin with an embrace of the other, as God does, rather than positing a polarized separation into warring factions. While being clear about the end being God's shalom, we also adopt the means to see others, not as

When politics is the fruit of mysticism, it takes root in the daily living of our lives.

enemies, but as those with gifts and wounds who yearn, whether consciously or not, to experience an unbounded love which calms their fears, shatters their illusions, and enlivens their souls.

In my view, the invitation to embark on such an inward spiritual journey is the only certain way I know to get beyond and beneath the siloed, polarized political culture of our time. We all need to wander in the wilderness before we pronounce our message.

E NGAGEMENT IN THE political process, broadly defined, is not an option. It's inevitable. For instance, in today's world, with devastating climate change, rural poverty, and immigration conflicts, what we have for lunch, where we eat, and how we get there all can have political consequences. When politics is the fruit of mysticism, it takes root in the daily living of our lives. It also often leads to direct political involvement, whether through voting, advocating, speaking, organizing, lobbying, or running for and holding elective political office. For all people of faith, the question is not whether to be "political," but how to do so with intentional awareness, commitment, and faithfulness to the vision and love which has claimed and called us.

From my experience as an assistant to a US Senator, a consultant to a White House advisory group, a long-time partner with an advocacy group for faith and justice (Sojourners), and a leader of a US denomination, here are three things I've learned:

1. **Always keep the end in clear view**. The political process constantly wants to shrink the horizon of what's possible. The person of faith wants to expand it, looking toward God's intended horizon. Always let that be your moral compass and remind those enmeshed in the political process how to envision the long-term goal.

2. **Compromise is not evil.** If the end for which we yearn is shaped by the hope of God's reign breaking into this world, we should learn to expect immediate outcomes that are imperfect. What's important are the direction and the sense of urgency. Are we moving toward the interdependent ends of justice, peace, and integrity of creation, with an imperative commitment, or are we retreating from them?

3. **Speak the language of religious faith.** Often people of faith engaging in politics assume that they must sanitize their vocabulary of spiritual language. Don't. Politicians expect religious people to share the basis of their convictions. That's not imposing this language on others, but being honest about our motives. It's fine to sound like a prophet when sharing a prophetic message.

During the healthcare debate this year, Jessi Bohon, a teacher in Tennessee, became politically engaged and went to a town hall meeting with her Representative in the House, Diane Black. Jessi got up and said, "As a Christian, my whole philosophy in life is to pull up the unfortunate. We are effectively punishing our sickest people." It was a conversation that went viral and served as a simple but powerful example of the political witness from a person of faith.

IN THIS ERA of Donald Trump's presidency, it's more important than ever for politics to emerge from mysticism. The late Edwin Friedman (1932–1996), author of *Generation to Generation*,[4] wrote perceptively about how the dysfunction in family systems can be applied to religious organizations and the wider life of society. We can become easily trapped, Friedman argued, in emotional reactivity, where the dysfunction of one person, including a key leader, provokes equally dysfunctional responses of anger, anxiety, and fear from others. The whole system is afflicted by a series of emotional dominoes. It takes the self-differentiated leadership of others, who know their emotional and spiritual center and are not hooked by the dysfunction of the system, to bring health, clarity, and wisdom.

Our present political order is as dysfunctional as any that I have seen in my lifetime. It's fueled by the President's own narcissistic wounds, but this infects the whole. Hopes and places of healing will depend on those who find a different and differentiated starting point. The necessary detachment from this ugly and injurious present political climate depends upon our inner attachment to the mystery of God's unbounded grace and divine, creative love. That is the foundation from which we can witness to truth, nurture community, and build essential bonds of solidarity with those who suffer. More than ever, politics which offers redemptive hope will begin with mysticism. •

Confessions of a Preacher in the Borderlands

By Rachel M. Srubas

O N April 24, 2010, I attended a parliamentary meeting of Presbyterian leaders in Tucson, Arizona, where I live. I may have been the only pastor present for whom the day carried ancestral significance. April 24 marks the anniversary of the Armenian Genocide, begun in Turkey in 1915. Some of my maternal ancestors were among the estimated one million Armenians exterminated in Turkey. Others managed to flee and resettle in the United States. "Who, after all, speaks today of the…Armenians?" Adolf Hitler asked this chilling rhetorical question in 1939 when presenting plans to invade Poland and exterminate the Poles.[1]

As we Presbyterians deliberated on matters important to our congregations, political outrage was erupting throughout the Southern Arizona borderlands with Mexico. Protestors' placards grimly punned, "Arizona: It's a Dry Hate." One day earlier, then-Governor of Arizona, Jan Brewer, had signed into law Senate Bill 1070. It became the United States' strictest immigration law and required local law enforcement officers making "any lawful contact" with a person "where reasonable suspicion exists that the person is an alien...to determine the immigration status of the person."[2] While Roman Catholic Bishops of Arizona had issued a moderately worded letter opposing the bill before it became law, once Brewer signed it, Cardinal Roger Mahony, Archbishop of the Los Angeles Diocese, blogged, "I can't imagine Arizonans now reverting to German Nazi and Russian Communist techniques whereby people are required to turn one another in to the authorities on any suspicion of documentation."[3] Paul Dobson, a twenty-year veteran of the Phoenix Police Department, posted a video on Facebook, calling the law "racist" and adding that it would "make me feel like a Nazi out there."[4]

At the church leaders' meeting, anxiety spiked when pastors known for their work with migrants' rights groups leafleted commissioners, urging us to oppose the law. One pastor literally wailed and gnashed his teeth as he spoke in favor of a motion that our judicatory denounce the law. While Robert's Rules of Order do not lend themselves well to public lamentation, Presbyterians do have a long history of political activism and resistance. Indeed, one of the "six great ends" of our church, as stated in its constitution, is "the promotion of social righteousness."[5]

Fully cognizant that, a century earlier, my ancestors had suffered grave injustices stemming from xenophobic policies, I suppressed my queasiness, stood, and spoke against the motion. I recognized the biblical and moral reasons for it, but I argued that we needed more time to process a law that had been signed fewer than twenty-four hours earlier. Most of us were only then learning about the legislation. I was mindful of my congregants, predominantly white middle-class suburban retirees, some of whom believed (mistakenly) that separation of church and state means the church must never take a public stand on legislative matters.

While I stated—and believed—that more education was needed before the regional church body could take informed collective action, I was also afraid of losing my job. I feared one congregant in particular, who, five years earlier, had played a leading role in the ouster of the congregation's previous pastor. Among her other complaints, she had disapproved of his involvement in border ministries. German-born during World War II, she had immigrated to the United States as a child in the early 1950s—a traumatizing experience for her. In the late 1990s, she and her American-born husband had helped to found, and substantially fund, our congregation. They held positions of influence as well as unchristian views on undocumented migrants. He once sat in my church office and told me, "If I ever saw illegals crossing the border, I'd shoot them on sight."

Somehow, I had to try to lead not only these people in following Jesus, but also congregants in the clear but quieter majority. Most held moderate-to-progressive perspectives on undocumented migrants who trek through the sometimes-blistering Arizona desert to search for economic opportunity. Too often, they die trying. While our regional church judicatory's formal denunciation of Arizona's new "show me your papers" policy might have exerted a little moral pressure on law-makers, it also might have subjected pastors like me to the mistrust of some congregants whose reactive sabotage could ruin our ministries and mental health. In short, I voiced an opinion based as much on my own fear as on pastoral realism, and I incurred a withering public rebuttal from one clergy colleague.

Then another pastor rose to speak. He opposed the motion. Although his own spouse had fled war-ravaged Central America during the 1980s and entered the US illegally as a child, he did not believe the church judicatory was ready to publicly denounce the new immigration law. He invoked one of the ordination vows that ministers of our denomination make: "to further the peace, unity, and purity of the church."[6] He wasn't willing to subject his already hurting flock to political controversy. Like me, he too probably wanted to hold on to his job.

The motion failed. By some moral estimates, we church leaders failed too. Arizona's immigration law faced intensive legal challenges and, in 2016, the state announced that local law enforcement officers would no longer be required to determine the immigration status of suspected undocumented people. The decision was a victory not only for borderlands families, but even more for Christ, in whom no dualistic categories prevail. Soon, however, political barriers were fortified when a man who touted border wall-building became the US President. The fractious days surrounding his election had been fore-shadowed by many tensions, including those within Arizona in 2010.

To the powerful congregants who
had once scared me out of preaching
prophetically, I announced, in effect,
that I would no longer kowtow
to them.

One Sunday in May of that year, two weeks after the anxious judicatory meeting, I preached into the tensions, urging my congregants to think biblically about immigration. I was trying to foster the very reflection I had argued was necessary before political action could wisely be taken. I was also attempting to bring some faithful, nonpartisan nuance to the process. To that end, I quoted biblical scholar Walter Brueggemann's insight: "Ideology is the self-deceiving practice of . . . taking 'my truth' for the truth."[7] But I could not pretend neutrality. By this time, I had studied Arizona's new immigration law and was convinced it sanctioned racial profiling and violated the unconditional love of Jesus Christ for all people. In the sermon, I praised faith groups that had denounced the law for such reasons.

Preachers have reasons, both acknowledged and unconscious, for what we preach. Sometimes we appear to contradict ourselves when, in reality, our minds have changed. To undergo a change of mind is, in essence, to repent. My sermon was an act of repentance. Having worked to keep the church judicatory from publicly opposing the immigration law, I now criticized the law from the pulpit. In doing so, I surfaced a fault line within the internal politics of my congregation. To the powerful congregants who had once scared me out of preaching prophetically, I announced, in effect, that I would no longer kowtow to them. This wasn't all bravery and righteousness on my part. Enough naïveté and self-deception were also in play that when a dozen congregants (among them those who had forced the previous pastor's resignation) staged a walkout, I was stunned.

Their protest was more passive-aggressive than theatrical. They waited until after the service of worship and orchestrated a boycott over brunch. Then the man who had pledged to gun down "illegals" was dispatched to my office. He said, "I'm not good at this"—but he was good enough. I got the message: Either I retract the sermon and its liberal subtext, or the church would lose a dozen or more charter members. With a membership of about 140, this would represent nearly ten percent of the congregation.

In as pastoral a tone as I could muster, I refused to take back the sermon. The man issuing the ultimatum countered plaintively, "They're calling us Nazis." He was speaking of those protesting Arizona's stringent new immigration law, but I sensed displacement at work. "They" meant "you." "Us" included his German émigré wife, whose parents, it was not outlandish to imagine, may once have affiliated with the political party of the Third Reich.

Writing such words feels dangerous, but denying their possible veracity seems more so. The delusion of innocence can keep whole societies from admitting their wrongs, as the Republic of Turkey demonstrates in persistently denying the Armenian Genocide perpetrated by its twentieth-century founders. When John Calvin (1509–1564), theological parent of the Presbyterians, pointed out the "total depravity" of our species, he meant to eliminate any supposed soteriological loophole; we're all thoroughly complicit in evil, he argued, and God alone can save us. In Calvin's anthropologically pessimistic yet doxological view, we must admit the worst about ourselves if we are to rejoice in our redemption by a surpassingly gracious God. Like it or not, this is a historic, foundational premise of the little church where I preached what I came to think of (with an odd combination of self-effacement and hubris) as "the sermon that would live in infamy."

The departure of the congregation's disgruntled dozen made for a rocky year. Once-occupied seats in the church's intimate sanctuary sat glaringly empty. Close friends of those who had left the church struggled with divided loyalties, in some cases lashing out at me, in others lavishing affection, as if to prove there were no hard feelings.

Over time, transformation occurred. Newer congregants stepped into leadership positions previously unavailable to them. At the church door, following worship one Sunday, a respected charter member looked me squarely in the eye and made an elliptical but laden remark: "Good work. It's better now." The measurable signs that it was in fact better now included a significant increase in financial pledges supporting the congregation's operating budget and mission commitments. The latter came to include our loving sponsorship of

Congolese and Syrian refugee families. Since before the previous pastor's resignation, the congregation had served and sold fair-trade coffee produced in a Presbyterian binational cooperative just over the US-Mexico border. The congregation set and met higher coffee-sales goals and increased its support of other borderlands ministries. They also gave me a raise and, eventually, a three-month sabbatical.

The time off allowed me to make an ancestral pilgrimage to Turkey, one year before the Armenian Genocide's centenary. En route to Istanbul, I spent a week in Berlin, Germany. On an overcast Ash Wednesday morning, I visited Berlin's Monument to the Murdered Jews of Europe. There, over an entire city block, an uneven concrete foundation undulates disconcertingly underfoot, giving rise to corridors of boxy stones, seeming sarcophagi. Cement staircases descend to steel doors that would open to brick walls if they could be opened at all.

In a restaurant booth, I drank cup after cup of tea and read the memoir of an Auschwitz survivor. He recalled the musical performances that inmates managed to present for their own entertainment and that of the captors who would send them to their deaths. He remembered the guileless blue summer sky beyond the reach of the camp's demonic miseries.

That evening, I made my way to an English-language liturgy in a cavernous church so chilly the ushers handed out blankets along with worship bulletins. A pastor in a purple stole read from the Book of Isaiah: "Yet day after day they seek me and delight to know my ways, as if they were a nation that practiced righteousness and did not forsake the ordinance of their God" (58:2a, NRSV). As choristers harmonized our contrition, a multinational smattering of shivering Anglophones went forward to receive sooty cruciform smudges on the forehead. Defaced, I returned to my pew, wrapped a loaner blanket around me, and steeled myself to travel on to yet another country of forsaken people. •

A Moment for Something More Soulful Than Politics

By *Joan D. Chittister, OSB*

I N THE PRESIDENTIAL primary of 2016, Donald Trump scorned Senator John McCain's heralded heroic captivity during the Vietnam War. "He was a war hero because he was captured," Trump said. "I believe *perhaps* he is a war hero." He then went on: "I like people who weren't captured."[1] The attack stunned the nation. The young naval aviator, Lieutenant Commander John McCain, tortured and permanently disabled, stood up to the whole North Vietnamese system. Offered release, McCain refused to take it until the rest of the squadron would be released, as well. It was four more years before that happened.

In 2017, as the acme of the GOP attempt to repeal President Barack Obama's signature legislation on healthcare without proposing an acceptable replacement, two women senators–Susan Collins and Lisa Murkowski–and John McCain voted against such an irresponsible legislative maneuver. The repeal attempt went down to defeat by three heroes who confronted our own system with truth and courage.

On that day, President Trump found himself faced with a clear picture of what heroes really are–both in captivity and beyond. Heroes are those who are free enough internally to face any amount of external pressure for the sake of the greater good.

Heroism is not a rare event. In fact, it is a given.

In every life there is a crossover moment, after which a person will never be the same again. Somewhere, somehow the challenge comes that sets us on a different path: the path of purpose, the path of integrity, the path of transcendence that lifts us–heart, mind, and soul–above the pitiable level of the comfortable and the mundane.

It is the moment at which transcending the mediocre, the conventional, the pedestrian, becomes more impacting, more holy-making than any amount of beige-colored political success.

As a culture, we may have come to that point. As a people, we are at a crossover moment. It is a call to all of us to be our best, our least superficial, our most serious about what it means to be a Christian as well as a citizen.

The system we have, divided from itself–separation of church and state–important as it is in a pluralistic state, must nevertheless be compatible in us or we may never really be One, never be united as a people, ever again.

Mark Twain may have put it best. "The only rational patriotism," he writes, "is loyalty to the Nation ALL the time, loyalty to the Government when it deserves it."[2] Aye, there's the rub.

As Shakespeare's Hamlet wrestles with the demands of conscience in the face of the growing crises of the kingdom, he weighs the effects of two possible approaches. He can confront the situation at the heart of the problem. He can unmask the perfidy that threatens to steal his country away from him. Or, fearful of the consequences of public opposition, he can simply ignore it, minimize it, go to sleep, ignore it . . . "and by a sleep to say we end the heartache."[3]

Who doesn't understand the dilemma? The political world is a stockpile of polar opposites. Which option shall we ourselves choose–

to confront a disorderly system or to simply go along to get along?

We can speak up as our democracy begins to break down before our eyes and bear the public stress that comes with that. Or, in our own case, in this time, we too can "sleep through it." We can do everything possible to avoid the situation. We can hope that, at least eventually, everything will just die down on its own without our having to do something about it. After all, the cure could indeed be worse than the disease.

Indeed, a Hamlet wails in us all: "Aye, there's the rub."

The truth is that we know the depth of our own situation only too well these days. We're in it, after all. Even to write about it here seems almost surreal. I keep waiting to wake up again in a nice, orderly America: long great; definitely grown; a paragon of professional, presidential civility; and certainly a beacon to many.

Instead, I'm caught in a maelstrom of the unexpected:

- A foreign government has inserted itself into our democracy in an attempt to upset the credibility as well as the integrity of the democratic system itself.

- The popular vote–the majority choice of the voters–does not assure an election.

- The President of the country is also its Tweeter-in-chief and the dominant debaser, "de-meaner," and prevaricator of the country, as well.

- Meanwhile, presidency and monarchy are being confused while people stand helplessly by as the corpse of civil liberty sinks into a national grave.

- Even as I write, the self-proclaimed sexual-predator President is insulting his own Attorney General in public, just one more person in a long line of personal casualties. Meanwhile, we go on trying to convince our children not to bully anyone and not to give in to it themselves.

- Meanwhile, the Congress of the United States dithers with people's lives in the hope of scoring political points while universal healthcare, education, cyber security, climate change, and international affairs take second place to the presidential reality show and local soap operas.

- Furthermore, whatever issues of constitutionality may be created by any of these things, the president apparently thinks that he can solve the problems by pardoning himself.

Worst of all, all this chaos, political instability, and lack of experience was demonstrated in living color in the process called a primary. In that standard political ritual, with over a dozen candidates to choose from, if the voting public itself had heeded the obvious, such a political debacle could have been avoided.

The question is, why didn't they heed the obvious? And, if they did, why did they ignore the implications for the country? After all, "they" is "we"; we did this to ourselves.

Even more important, where in the midst of such polarization and national disunity is even the hope of *oneing*, of integrating the social with what we say are our spiritual selves? Where is the missing link between the spiritual life and civic life? Where is the tie between religion and politics in a time when "God bless America" is a national creed but "America First" has become its god?

Even the ghost of an answer makes serious spiritual demands on us all: To heal such division means that we are obliged to search out and identify our own personal value system. It requires us to admit to ourselves what it is that really drives our individual social decisions, our votes, our political alliances. Is it the need to look powerful? The desire for personal control? The hope to cash in on the quick fixes or profit from the petty skimming? The need to be approved of by the titled class? Do we have the courage to confront the debased with the ideal—even in the face of ridicule and recrimination—or is cowardice our secret spiritual sickness? In that case, our national health can only get worse.

A national cure also surely demands that we begin to see tradition as a call to return to the best of the past, not a burden to be overcome in order to secure the best of the present. It is the sense of a commonly held tradition of the common good—once a strong part of the American past—that we clearly lack in the present. We have searched for months to find some senators, some representatives, even a few

Politics—government—does not exist for itself and, if it does, that is precisely when it becomes at least death-dealing if not entirely evil.

political leaders who themselves were sufficiently beyond petty party differences to care enough to speak for us all. Instead, such profiles in courage have been rare on the political ground. And so politics has become the problem rather than part of the answer to the national division that plagues us.

Any answer that can possibly heal the national fissure must surely enable us to see conservatism as the anchor of society and, at the same time, to welcome liberalism as the path to the future that is already here.

Most of all, a real answer to such bickering and character assassination will necessitate that we make "Love one another as I have loved you" (see John 13:34) the foundation of national respect, the standard of our national discernment, the bedrock of both our personal relationships and a civilized society.

To make those spiritual concepts a real part of life and so to bring this country together again, at least five issues are paramount:

- First, partisan politics, a relatively new concept in national politics, has to be seen for what it is: a fungus on the democratic system that chokes its growth and smothers its oxygen. Partisan politics—the notion that the herd mentality is more important to democracy than individual conscience and personal responsibility for the civil system—has to end. Otherwise, the very keepers of the kingdom will have sliced and diced the political system into national uselessness.

- Second, we must return to a fundamental American conservative posture. We must remember that the Constitution is more important than the politics or the politicians of the moment. To manipulate voting blocks, to gerrymander the system, to intimidate a voting population into staying away from the polls for the sake of party dominance is not government. It is treason.

- Third, we must remember that civil discourse is the pillar of democracy. The deterioration of public discussion to the level of street talk—led, in this case, by the president himself—limits thinking and invites name-calling. The inherent value of the issue then disappears in a flame and flash of irrationality and national narcissism. At that point, all objectivity goes to dust and drains a democracy of its essential components: fearlessness and respect for the other.

- Fourth, we must realize that, to be an effective country, we must become as much citizens of the world as we are citizens of this nation. There is no country anymore that can stand alone—not even us, as global economics and the questions of national security so clearly show.

- Fifth, to be *one*, we don't need one party, one program, one set of policies. What could be duller, more stagnant, more destructive of the soulfulness it takes to create and preserve the best of the human enterprise than such a narrow-minded view of planetary life? What we need is one heart for the world at large, a single-minded commitment to this "more perfect union," and one national soul, large enough to listen to one another for the sake of the planet—for the sake of us all.

So, WHERE CAN we look for *oneing* in the political arena? Only within the confines of our own hearts. Politics—government—does not exist for itself and, if it does, that is precisely when it becomes at least death-dealing if not entirely evil. Nation-states and empires have all "died the death" in the wake of such power run amuck, of such distortion of human community.

In the end, politics is nothing more than an instrument of social good and human development. It is meant to be the right arm of those whose souls have melted into God. It is to be the living breath of those who say they are religious people and patriotic citizens—a link to personal faith.

This current period of politics, instead, flirts with the notion of being the security of the secure, the enrichment of the rich. In the name of personal responsibility, it disdains those who cannot sustain themselves with dignity in a world in transition from the industrial revolution to the technological revolution.

Instead, it sets out to divorce itself from the very values that made this country great: the democratic system and the Judeo-Christian values it has embodied.

The democratic system, as originally conceived, upholds a vision that links "care for widows and children" with a commitment to provide food stamps and a living wage for families under stress.

It embodies the soul of a nation that considers the right to breathe clean air and drink clean water, to save wetlands and reduce fossil fuels, to be a responsibility of America's own Environmental Protection Agency.

It includes the love for all of God's creation that links Jesus' cure of Jairus' daughter (see Matthew 9:18–25) and the man born blind (see John 9) with the moral obligation to provide healthcare and social services to all of us, not simply to some.

It embraces the courage of the Samaritan to reach out to the foreigner (see Luke 10:25–37) that made this country open arms toward an immigrant world.

In fact, it is the strength of the link between religion and politics that will determine both the quality of our politics and the authenticity of our religion.

The echo of Martin Luther King, Jr., can be heard again—this time, perhaps, with more of the warning of the prophet than the hope of the spiritually naïve. King wrote, "Any religion that professes to be concerned with the souls of men and is not concerned with the slums that damn them, the economic conditions that strangle them, and the social conditions that cripple them, is a spiritually moribund religion in need of new blood."[4]

It is between those two poles—real religion and genuine patriotism—that the Hamlet in all of us is now challenged to *one* our democratic ideals with the best of our religions, the gold standard of our souls.

To phrase Hamlet more directly, it is time for us to wake up. Sleeping through this sad American moment will never enable us to become again who we have so often said we are. •

A Meditation on Hope and Fear

By *Lee Staman*

Fear operates as an appetite or an addiction. You can never be safe enough.

—Marilynne Robinson

For if you find hope in the ground of history, you are united with the great prophets who were able to look into the depth of their times, who tried to escape it, because they could not stand the horror of their visions, and who yet had the strength to look to an even deeper level and there to discover hope.

—Paul Tillich

I

R ELIGION AND POLITICS. They are not to be discussed in polite company. They arouse strong feelings, sometimes visceral reactions. I would wager that each of us has a story about one or both and how our views have changed or been confirmed, or maybe we've decided to take a break from them. It is probably rare to find someone that does not take a firm stance on some topic related to religion and politics. Religion, what Abraham Joshua Heschel (1907–1972) calls the "answer to ultimate questions,"[1] reflects what we think about that which is greater than us. And politics, how we interact with our community of people, reflects how we seek to govern and be governed.

It is not my purpose or desire to explore all aspects of how religion and politics have engaged one another throughout history. There are plentiful arguments to be made around their separation, instances in which the two have worked hand-in-hand for the betterment of those involved, and the tragedies when one or both are misused toward disastrous ends. Religion and politics impact our daily lives; for better or worse, they have the ability to instill fear and inspire hope. Of politics, Thomas Merton (1915–1968) said,

> We will never get anywhere unless we can accept the fact that politics is an inextricable tangle of good and evil motives in which, perhaps, the evil predominate but where one must continue to hope doggedly in what little good can still be found.[2]

It is this idea of hope in the midst of fear that I wish to explore here, that, "even if the future of humanity and the earth looks dark, to hope means to live and survive, and to work and fight for the life of creation."[3]

II

I AM THE FATHER of two boys. The elder is two while the younger is four months old. If there is an embodiment of hope, it is in our children. If there is an embodiment of fear, it is also in our children. I have found that I can be on an edge that teeters between my hope for their lives and the fear of the known and unknown that exists in life. Hope and fear both live in the not-yet.

One unknown for their lives revolves around the question of how we will introduce religion into their lives. With this, I am forced to think back on my own upbringing with regard to religion. The Christianity in which I was schooled early on was one that moved largely in fear and blended with politics into a constant vigil for signs of the end times. Hope was that a pre-tribulation rapture would rescue all true Christians from the hell on earth of the tribulation period. The daily fear—that you were somehow not one of those that would be caught up because you did not believe with all your heart and mind—made religion a terrifying blend of hope and fear. Anthony Kelly's insight into hope, specifically when future-obsessed, would have been useful: "In contrast to all forms of impatient apocalyptic prediction—religious or secular—hope offers no detailed knowledge of the future."[4] A misplaced future hope was made possible because of a present fear.

Paradoxically, hope itself can seem to be fear-inducing. We are left holding onto something that is not-yet, something that we can never seem to grasp, but rely on; "hope moves in darkness,"[5] as Kelly said. I think that, for a lot of people, the unknown sparks fear but very little hope. In a sense, fear is immediate gratification. We encounter the unknown and fear is a reliable partner, something we have known before—often unwanted, but there nonetheless. Hope is not something that occurs to us naturally, "because we don't bring this true hope with us from birth, and because our experiences of life may perhaps make us wise but not necessarily hopeful, we have to go out to learn hope."[6]

III

A<small>T FIRST, WE</small> might cultivate an optimistic outlook, which is certainly good, in and of itself, but it is not hope. Krista Tippett puts it this way: "Hope is distinct, in my mind, from optimism or idealism. It has nothing to do with wishing. It references reality at every turn and reveres truth."[7] Again, Kelly: "Hope is not mere wishing for something more. It is a conduct of life.... Hope anticipates a future fulfillment that is yet to be given."[8] Wishful thinking, idealism, dreams of a future utopia do not have the same grounding as hope. The great German theologian, Jürgen Moltmann, perhaps best known for his work on the theology of hope, helps us understand utopian (literally "no-place") thinking:

Hope and the kind of thinking that goes with it consequently cannot submit to the reproach of being utopian, for they do not strive after things that have "no place," but after things that have "no place yet" but can acquire one.[9]

This is the now but not-yet of hope and it is not subject to the whims and fleeting nature of mere optimism. Heschel, in good apophatic tradition, tells us that, "Hope is not cheerfulness, a temperamental confidence that all will turn out for the best. It is not an inclination to be guided by illusions rather than by facts. Hope is a conviction, rooted in trust."[10]

Fear is easily taught and easily taken in. We are told many things in the realms of both politics and religion and, in many cases, what we are told is that this or that will be taken from us, either presently or in some future time. We learn that we should be afraid of these things and I admit that there are many things–especially now, with children–of which I am afraid, but I can also make a daily choice to practice hope. In Hesiod's poem, *Works and Days* (lines 60–105), he touches on the mythological story of Pandora's Box. It is well-known how Pandora opened the box and let out all the evils of the world but that Elpis, the goddess of hope, was left inside the box. It is unclear in Hesiod's poem why hope did not fly out and I love that ambiguity: that hope is not something we fully experience, even when all other evils are loosed. Anthony Kelly offers up this description: "Hope is not allowed to rest in any imagination drawn from the present sphere of human experience … hope must learn to live with not only not-understanding and not-representing but also with a certain not-willing."[11] Hope is hard work. It is meant to be cultivated, tended to on a regular basis. It is an activity.

In his work *Faith, Hope, Love*, the German philosopher Josef Pieper (1904–1997) talks about our *status viatoris*, or "our condition or state of being on the way."[12] Our movement through life is just that–movement. Physically, spiritually, our whole being moves. Hope keeps things moving, hope is now but not-yet. Heschel stresses the need for attentiveness when he says, "Hope cannot stand alone. It must be morally substantiated, faithfully attended. It must not lose the element of constancy and the intensity of expectancy."[13] Pieper again speaks paradoxically of hope as the "absence of fulfillment and the orientation toward fulfillment."[14]

Hope is hard work.
It is meant to be cultivated,
tended to on a regular basis.
It is an activity.

Fear stagnates; it hinders and slows our movement. Our journey seems beset on all sides when fear replaces our vision of hope. The not-yet of hope, that warming vision and lifeblood, becomes the seemingly tangible cold taste of fear in our mouths. The daily focus of what we would accomplish—again, movement—is stopped in its tracks and we follow fear into a swamp. The Roman philosopher Seneca (4 BCE–65 CE) saw hope and fear as partners:

> They are bound up with one another, unconnected as they may seem. Widely different though they are, the two of them march in unison like a prisoner and the escort he is handcuffed to. Fear keeps pace with hope. Nor does their so moving together surprise me; both belong to a mind in suspense, to a mind in a state of anxiety through looking into the future. Both are mainly due to projecting our thoughts far ahead of us instead of adapting ourselves to the present.[15]

Seneca saw both as resulting from either desires that led to fear or as the curse of human foresight that leads to hope. For Seneca, hope and fear were distractions that kept us from the task at hand; why be tormented by things past and fearful of things future?

IV

I HAVE TO RESPECTFULLY disagree with the famous Stoic. I agree that fear keeps pace with hope. Often the thing hoped for can become riddled with fear over time. But, as Ernst Bloch (1885–1977) asserts, "Hope, superior to fear, is neither passive like the latter, nor locked into nothingness. The emotion of hope goes out of itself, makes people broad instead of confining them."[16] I have to believe that Bloch is correct, that hope makes us broad, that it releases us from the daily confines in which we can find ourselves. This idea that hope goes out from itself is beautiful to me. It makes me think of the communal aspects of hope and how a hope shared is greater than one kept to ourselves.

Fear seems to narrow everything. We experience it so deeply and it feels as though it closes our senses, creating a tunnel vision that only sees the fear at hand. Hope opens our hearts and minds. It shows us worlds that could be, but,

> To hope does not mean to know the future, but rather to be open, in an attitude of spiritual childhood, to accepting it as a gift. But this gift is accepted in the negation of injustice, in the protest against trampled human rights, and in the struggle for peace and fellowship. Thus hope fulfills a mobilizing and liberating function in history.[17]

It makes us aware of injustice, oppression, and fear—each the antithesis of hope. The practical work of hope,

> Inspires a moral conversion.... The moral dimension of hope challenges the politics of its time, national and international, to look beyond their natural alliances with power and wealth.... Most of all, hope allies itself with the hopeless, the exhausted, the forgotten, whom official history has relegated to the margins of worthlessness.[18]

Here, hope is instructive. It shows us what work must be done, and be done daily. In Merton's work, *No Man Is an Island*, he says, "Hope empties our hands in order that we may work with them. It shows us that we have something to work for, and teaches us how to work for it."[19]

Yet, this is often the hardship that hope places upon us. More often than not, we are not fated to see the realization of hope. Reinhold Niebuhr (1892–1971) makes this point: "Nothing that is worth doing can be achieved in our lifetime; therefore we must be saved by hope."[20] This should not be disheartening, but should spur a greater awareness of the daily tasks that can be done in hope.

V

L IVING HOPE IS defiant."[21] I have found myself returning to and being inspired by this powerful statement by Kelly. I feel as though it encapsulates what is essential in hope. It is not something just for the future, it is alive now, and it is not merely a fleeting emotional reaction to fear in life, it is audacious.

When I think about the future into which my boys will live, I try to remember to ground the hope I have for them in the present. That edge of which I spoke I know now to be the ambiguity and uneasiness that comes with living in the not-yet of hope. The unknown creates a deep emptiness inside that I must replenish daily with something that is both ephemeral and unwavering: hope. •

Reading the Beatitudes Under Executive Order 13767

By Rose Marie Berger

O UTSIDE, A HELICOPTER circles this DC neighborhood, a dog barks anxiously in the alley. Inside, a woman sits in a straight-backed chair, reading the Beatitudes. She adjusts her glasses. *"Bienaventurados los que lloran, porque ellos recibirán consolación."* Blessed are those who mourn, for they will be comforted. "It's a beautiful prayer," she says.

My neighbor Lola cleans office buildings during the week, takes English classes on Saturdays, goes to Mass on Sundays. Her husband operates a jackhammer for a construction crew. On the "Day Without an Immigrant," Lola's boss said, because it wasn't organized by the union, workers should not stay home. So she went to work. Her husband stayed home. "We have to stand together," he said.

Lola and her husband sometimes share their one-bedroom apartment with a man who was their neighbor in El Salvador. He works days, nights, weekends. He sleeps on a mattress in their main room for a few hours in the afternoon. Lola leaves *pupusas* for him, wrapped and warm. Sometimes he drinks too much, turns up the radio, dances. They quiet him so he doesn't disturb the neighbors. He feels safe there.

A few miles from Lola's apartment, Immigration and Customs Enforcement raided Rising Hope United Methodist Church (under President Obama, such "sensitive locations" were considered off-limits except in extreme cases). Men were rounded up as they left the church's hypothermia shelter. They were detained and effectively "disappeared," since church members have been unable to get any information about them from Immigration and Customs Enforcement (ICE) officials.

A few of Lola's neighbors have attended meetings to learn what to do when ICE agents come to one's home or work. They learn the differences between ICE paperwork that does not allow entry into a home and an official warrant, signed by a judge, that does. They learn how to sign over power of attorney to someone for the care of their children, should the parents be suddenly apprehended.

One of Lola's neighbors believes ICE only patrols certain "federal" highways and has an elaborate route mapped out for getting to and from work. This is dangerously untrue—but in a slow-motion crisis, rumors fly and false hope is found in a thousand Facebook posts.

Five days after his inauguration, Mr. Trump announced that it would be his policy going forward to "secure the southern border of the United States through the immediate construction of a physical wall" and "detain individuals apprehended on suspicion of violating Federal or State law" (Executive Order 13767). While the first is primarily political theater and another reallocation of taxpayer funds to private industry, the second is tearing apart families and neighborhoods. And churches are defending their mixed immigration-status communities by reasserting their ancient, biblical "right of sanctuary"— that a consecrated place may offer protection to those fleeing justice or persecution. In the 1980s, American churches offered safe, but illegal,

False hope is found in a thousand Facebook posts.

passage to people fleeing death squads in El Salvador. Today churches are shielding from deportation those already in the United States.

In March, twenty blocks from Lola's apartment, seventeen religious traditions launched the District, Maryland, and Virginia Sanctuary Congregation Network. Metropolitan AME Church's pastor, Rev. William H. Lamar IV, spoke at the press conference. "People ask why we stand with immigrants," he said. "Because black bodies have been assaulted since we first came to the States," he replied. "What we know is that if we are silent when brown bodies are assaulted, when gay bodies are assaulted, when trans bodies are assaulted, when female bodies are assaulted, then all of us remain imprisoned and in bondage."

"*Bienaventurados los que tienen hambre y sed de justicia,*" reads Lola, "*porque ellos serán saciados.*" Blessed are those who hunger and thirst for justice, for they will be satisfied. It is a beautiful prayer. •

Reprinted from Sojourners *magazine, June 2017, with permission of the author. sojo.net.*

For Catherine, the path toward discernment, by which one may understand the impact of one's actions on the world, begins in the knowledge of self.

common word in Western languages—French *même*, English *same*.[4] This identity recognizes the sameness of a human individual as time goes on, and especially in the manner of uninterrupted continuity (among others characteristics), that is, continuity of identity over time such that, even with large changes, a thing (or a person) can still be identified as being the same.[5] The only experience that seems to challenge this sameness is time itself, which, Ricœur states, "is a factor of dissemblance, of divergence, of difference" from what came before.[6] This is solved, however, using the notion of substance formulated by Immanuel Kant (1724–1804) as a "category of relation" by which a thing (in itself) may be related to its perceiver. This allows Ricœur to assert the existential sameness of the thing over the course of time. One may conceive of change happening to something, but the change does not really take place.[7]

For Catherine to assert the need for self-knowledge also implies that, for her, there is a part of oneself that one does not know, and is, in fact, wholly unknown. It is an entirely different thing, however, to make the case that the content of the identity that is currently unknown perseveres through time. D'Urso points out a few of the characteristics of self-knowledge as Catherine writes about it. He says, "knowledge at times is an interior grace, a light, a realistic consideration of one's own nothingness as a creature and sinner in general; …sometimes, it is the very act of self-humiliation, i.e., to recognize and to confess one's own misery."[8] Further, Bernard McGinn tells us that Catherine's idea of self-knowledge is the "awareness of the fact that we were created in God's image and likeness through divine love, but that we have soiled our created beauty by sin."[9] This is the content of self-knowledge to which all human persons must come, and is established as an anthropological claim. This knowledge of the human person would, then, persist, not only through space (that is, among persons from Catherine's own era) but also through time and, thus, the human person in general may be recognized as such through the uninterrupted continuation of this identity from person to person.

It is in this cell of self-knowledge that one encounters this permanent self that God knows, as Catherine points out: "she knows all that she is and every gift she has is from [God], not from herself."[10] The creature, according to Catherine, is always contingent before its Creator.[11] Without the Creator, as true self-knowledge teaches, the creature is nothing; she has no dignity, and "through no merit of hers but by his creation she is the image of God."[12] She also comes to know her own imperfection, which is understood to be the cause of, but not the same as, the sins that one commits in the world.[13] Finally, this self-knowledge grants that one may "find humility and hatred for [one's] sensual passions, recognizing the perverse law that is bound up in [one's] members, and is always fighting against the spirit."[14] These, for Catherine, are anthropological laws, known only when one enters the cell of self-knowledge.

The *ipse*-identity is entirely opposite that of the *idem*. Characterized by otherness, distinction, and diversity, "*ipse* implies no assertion concerning some unchanging core of the personality."[15] This identity is a reminder that "the person of whom we are speaking, and the agent on whom the action depends have a history, are their own history."[16] This is seen best, for Ricœur, in the concept of habit, in that habits are formed and become part of that which allows one to be recognized; that is, character. The self that acts in the world, and thus is changed by its actions, takes its place as distinct from the *idem*-identity in the human experience and finds its fullest meaning in an individual acting within the world. But, it is through the formation of habits, according to Ricœur, that this "acting-self" overlaps with the one that is permanent.[17]

For Catherine, the human person is not only inherently sinful, but is also necessarily social. Throughout her *Dialogue*, she reminds her reader of this reality and its implications. McGinn speaks of this in his own reading of her works as well, saying that "Catherine insists on the social character of sin, both the inherited sin of Adam and our own sinning. For her, every act of sin against God involves also a sin against our neighbor."[18] Catherine herself offers a confession of this toward the beginning of the *Dialogue*: "O eternal Father, I accuse myself before you, asking that you punish my sins in this life. And since I by my sins am the cause of the sufferings my neighbors must endure, I beg you in mercy to punish me for them."[19]

The building of a personal history, as Ricœur attributes it to the *ipse*-identity, relies on the formation of habits, which eventually become those characteristics by which a person is recognized. For Catherine, this happens on the path either to virtue or vice. "Open your mind's eye," God says to her, "and look at those who drown by their own choice, and see how low they have fallen by their sins."[20] The habits that the "servants and slaves of sin" have in their lifetime formed within themselves have been, as Ricœur would say, internalized; these persons have become that which they conceived in their hearts.[21] Likewise, virtue has been internalized in those "souls who end in loving charity and are bound by love."[22] "It is the truth," Catherine says at the very beginning of the *Dialogue*, "that by love's affection the soul becomes another himself," that is, the soul *becomes* divine.[23]

Ricœur's notions of the two distinct identities within the self are present in Catherine as a distinction between the characteristics of a human person in general, and by nature, and the innovations of the individual human person through acting in the world. I arrived here by examining how Catherine understands the content of self-knowledge, which is itself an anthropology–the sinfulness and contingency inherent in the human condition. Since all human persons are expected to come to this knowledge, I asserted a sameness and an uninterrupted continuity therein. And, in the case of the latter, I looked especially at how the introduction of innovations to the self, that is, the formation of habits (of virtue or vice), leads to one being recognized by those habits. We cannot remain in this place, however. It is true that, for Catherine, the path toward discernment, by which one may understand the impact of one's actions on the world, begins in the knowledge of self;[24] yet she also believes that this knowledge alone will only end in confusion[25] and ultimately self-destruction since one would know oneself only in terms of immense sinfulness.

Bernard McGinn reminds us that, for Catherine, "the night knowledge of our own nothingness must be tempered with the day knowledge of God's goodness."[26] So, it is toward this that I now turn, and not simply the necessity of the knowledge of God, but what exactly the content of this knowledge is. "What is it about this knowledge of God that is so important?" is the question I address here, having in mind all the while the goal already stated: internal and external peace and tranquility, granted by the cooperation of the two distinct identities (persisting and changing) along with the God-within. True knowledge of the love of God alone grants one the ability to truly love the neighbor, acting in the habit of virtue rather than of vice.[27] In this, one enters upon the path of inner tranquility, since, (1) "you are your chief neighbor,"[28] and (2) virtue becomes internalized and becomes that by which one is recognized; similarly, external tranquility since the love of God will naturally lead to the love of neighbor.

Before addressing our primary question, however, it is necessary that I unpack briefly the assertion I made above, that knowledge of self alone will bring only confusion. There are a couple of reasons for this, according to Catherine. The first is the inherent sinfulness of humanity. The second is that the human person relies fully on God, not only for strength in acting for virtue, but even for one's very existence. As D'Urso states, "we are nothing by ourselves, having received everything, both our existence and our nature," and, "we can do nothing by ourselves if God does not give us the strength."[29] These things force us to realize that "sin reduces us to being less than nothing," for the divine image within us has been tainted by sin; the human person becomes less than she should be and so loses "the right to life in every sense."[30] With knowledge only of this, the human individual falls into slavish fear and, rather than being stripped of selfish love,[31] continues in the habit of acting in less than true love toward the neighbor. Thus, she remains confused about her actions and nurtures the identity of vice rather than virtue.

It is also the case for Catherine that self-knowledge alone may bring only hatred of self: "From her deep knowledge of herself, a holy justice gave birth to hatred and displeasure against herself, ashamed as she was of her imperfection, which seemed to be the cause of all the evils in the world."[32] This "holy justice" is granted only when self-knowledge is attained alongside knowledge of God; without this latter knowledge there is indeed hatred, but it leads nowhere. When one enters into God, however, one can "see the dignity and beauty of [God's] reasoning creature,"[33] the human person.

God, for Catherine, is so much more than the one who instills the human person with "holy justice" and holy hatred of self, more than the one upon whom, like the sea for the fish within it,[34] humanity relies for life and sustenance. God is the one who *loved* us into being. Her writings are filled with statements of the immensity of God's love. She tells her audience of the sinfulness of humanity but later follows with a reminder of God's immense and insane love for us, as McGinn describes: "For all her attacks on contemporary evils in the church and in Christendom at large, Catherine's overwhelming sense of God's goodness and 'mad love' for humanity give her writings a fundamental optimism."[35] This God is *pazzo d'amore*, made insane out of love for humanity. Through both self-knowledge and the knowledge of the love of God, one comes to know that, in the first place, "even your own existence comes not from yourself but from me," and, in the second, "for I loved you before you came into being. And in my unspeakable love for you I willed to create you anew in grace. So I washed you and made you a new creation in the blood that my only-begotten Son poured out with such burning love."[36] At the moment one is given knowledge of the immeasurable love of God for creation, one is able to say to God, as Catherine does, "With unimaginable love you looked upon your creatures within your very self, and you fell in love with us. So it was love that made you create us and give us being just so that we might taste your supreme eternal good."[37]

It is when one has come to know of
the love of God, and experience it,
that one can then begin to
love one's neighbors.

It is when one has come to know of the love of God, and experience it, that one can then begin to love one's neighbors: "Her loving charity benefits herself first of all, as I have told you, when she conceives that virtue from which she draws the life of grace. Blessed with this unitive love she reaches out in loving charity to the whole world's need for salvation."[38] One knows of God's love, and one is able to return the love to God always through one's neighbors, within oneself first, and then, among those outside of oneself, one works toward the goal of tranquility, and, developing the habit of virtue, one becomes divine just as God became human.

CONCLUSION

Catherine's goal of peace and tranquility, both within oneself and within the surrounding world, can be reached only through the mutual cooperation of three realities within the self. The first of these realities is understood especially through the anthropology that Catherine develops, by which the human person is understood as inherently sinful and contingent. The knowledge of this is not something that Catherine alone must come to, but something that all human persons must understand of themselves as it is characteristic of every human person. The second, the "acting-self," is known simply through action in the world, whether in virtue or vice. Through this self, one adopts an identity of either virtue or vice, depending on how it is that one has acted in the world. Without the knowledge of God, however, the process of coming to be identified with virtue, rather than vice, falls apart. Knowledge of self alone does not allow one to act willfully out of true love, and one remains confused. A truly willful act of love for God and for one's neighbor can come only from the knowledge of the love of God. •

Religion and Politics

By Simone Campbell, SSS

I LIVE AT THE intersection of politics and religion.

I am a Catholic Sister. I lead a faith-based lobby in Washington, DC. I have a contemplative practice that grounds who I am—and I am deep into the details of federal policy. It could not get more intersectional than this.

I am a member of the Sisters of Social Service, based in California. We were founded in 1923 in response to Pope Leo's encyclical *Rerum Novarum*, the foundation of Catholic Social Teaching. Our call is to do the "social mission of the Church." In Budapest, our foundress, Margaret Slachta, was the first woman in the Hungarian Parliament. So, from our founding, we have known that our faith takes us into the public square.

One of the documents that Margaret wrote for us is entitled, *From the Hermitage of the Desert to the Center of Life*. Her vision is that we are called to be "rooted in the Holy Spirit," grounded in a contemplative life, and "sent on unbroken roads, trusted with the problems of today and tomorrow." It is this vision that has flowered in my life and that of my community.

I currently lead NETWORK Lobby for Catholic Social Justice, based in Washington, DC. We were founded by forty-seven Catholic Sisters from various communities in 1971 and opened our doors in 1972. We lobby on Capitol Hill on issues of income and wealth disparity in our nation. We are working in seven policy areas to "Mend the Gaps." One hundred thousand of our supporters around the country join us in the daunting project of shaping federal legislation. We have gotten some notoriety for our Nuns on the Bus campaigns and our work on healthcare legislation. At NETWORK, we often say that our care for the common good is care for "the 100%" instead of the 99% or the 1% or any other number.

This all seems rather straightforward. Take the Gospel to the public square and work for the sake of those living in poverty. In *Evangelii Gaudium*, Pope Francis says, "Growth in justice requires more than economic growth, while presupposing such growth: it requires decisions, programs, mechanisms and processes specifically geared to a better distribution of income, the creation of sources of employment and an integral promotion of the poor which goes beyond a simple welfare mentality."[1] This is the twenty-first-century political challenge of our work–making faith alive in our rather messy politics.

My meditation practice has led me to see that God is alive in all. No one can be left out of my care. Therefore this political work is anchored in caring for those whom we lobby as well as those whose cause we champion. This was illustrated for me recently when I was with four of my colleagues lobbying a Republican Senator on healthcare legislation. I commented on the story of a constituent and asked her how her colleagues could turn their eyes away from the suffering and fear of their people. The conversation went on a bit, and then the senator came back to my question. She said that many of her colleagues controlled access for those with whom they met. They did not get close to the candid stories of their people. In fact, some did not see these constituents as "their people." Tears sprang to my eyes at her candor and the pain that keeps us sealed off from each other because of political partisanship. Compassion spills out of safe containers to flood our lives.

It is breaking my heart that some of these same politicians want to dismantle healthcare and force millions of our people off of healthcare

Faith has real consequences in the world...and these consequences involve politics.

they receive through the Affordable Care Act. Pope Francis is correct when he says that "health is not a consumer good, but a universal right, so access to health services cannot be a privilege."[2] Some in Congress want to take away healthcare coverage in order to make a partisan point. It is these members of Congress that I have a difficult time caring about. I would love to push them out of my care.

However, I find our position "for the 100%" requires an empathy that stretches my being beyond my imagining. Finding a way to not vilify or divide into "them" and "us" in today's federal politics goes against all of the pollsters' and pundits' advice and current custom. I too want to decry the current administration's policies and practices that demean so many and are tearing our nation apart.

So my contemplative practice is to attempt to sit open-handed and listen to the "wee small voice" that sometimes whispers ideas and ways forward. Following the conversation with the senator, I held her anguish in my silence. What came to me was a way to attempt to break through this wall that some have built around themselves, sealing them off from their constituents' pain and fears. As a consequence, we at NETWORK gathered pictures and stories of people from key states and delivered them to the healthcare policy staff of their states. We did this in order to make the reality of their constituents vivid before their eyes. I don't know if this made a dent in their wall of seeming indifference, but I know that it gave me and our organization the opportunity to exercise our care for the 100%—including senators who might vote against their constituents' interests.

My faith impels me into the public square. It is abundantly clear that Pope Francis is correct when he says that faith has real consequences in the world...and these consequences involve politics. *But*, what I find daunting and painful are the politics within my religion— the Roman Catholic Church.

Some of the leaders of our Catholic Church have staked out civil political positions on issues of abortion and gay marriage that are rigid and seemingly shaped in fear and anger. These positions have been identified as *the* Catholic position and are filled with judgment and condemnation. Not only that, they have been defined as the only positions about which Catholics are supposed to care.

When I was newly at NETWORK, I was going on the Hill to lobby about development aid for Iraqis in the aftermath of our 2003 invasion. While I had explained to the scheduler what we wanted to talk about with the staffer, the scheduler assumed that since I was *Sister* Simone that I wanted to talk about abortion. Therefore the appointment had been set with the staff member that covered abortion, not the one who handled international aid! It was straightened out after we briefly talked at cross purposes, but it underscored for me how "Catholic" and "anti-abortion" have been equated.

While we have worked at educating Capitol Hill staff about the broader issues we address, there is an additional consequence that at times overshadows our Gospel advocacy. Because of the extreme view of some Church leaders and their staffs, many Catholic institutions will not collaborate with any organization that has interaction with organizations that have a different view on these two defining, but narrow, issues. This is true even if abortion and LGBTQ rights are not the legislative issues at hand.

The Spirit has pushed us out of our comfort zone of acceptability in order to meet the needs of people we had not known were ours.

My prayer has led me to reject this rigidity as I have come to know that reflection on the Gospel leads to compassion. Compassion often leads to much more nuanced analysis, but nuance is not comfortable for those who feel the need to teach in absolutes and extremes. As an aside, I have a hunch that some in Church leadership think that enforcing the rules is the only option for spiritual leaders. Pope Francis has demonstrated another approach, but it has not penetrated some people's perspectives.

As I was preparing to write this piece, our organization was asked to be a co-sponsor of a campaign that included Planned Parenthood and NARAL (National Abortion and Reproductive Rights Action League). The campaign is one to protect Medicaid, which serves some of the most vulnerable people in our nation. Medicaid is the focus of much of our advocacy in the healthcare policy debate, so it would be natural to sign on. But Catholic institutional leaders (claiming the pro-life mantle) have labeled both Planned Parenthood and NARAL as the center of pro-choice abortion rights activism and a pariah in our society.

This invitation became "Exhibit A" of this Church-politics discussion.

My contemplative challenge is that I, as a Catholic who is committed to the dignity of all life, live at an intersection where these choices are not so clear-cut. I know that Planned Parenthood is the sole source of health services for many women throughout our nation. When I practiced family law in California, many of my clients used Planned Parenthood's services for their healthcare needs. A small percentage of Planned Parenthood's work is actual abortions. NARAL advocates for women's rights and expanding the capacity to have their voices heard. For me, both of these missions enhance the dignity of women's lives and further my pro-life stance of working for the dignity of all creation. So, after consultation with staff, we signed on to be a co-sponsor of an effort to protect Medicaid funding for low-income families.

This more nuanced approach comes out of my prayer and call to care for the 100%, but it does come at a price. Personally, for me, it has resulted in some institutional Church people attacking me for allegedly being pro-abortion. Our organization has been cited by Rome as promoting "radical feminist themes incompatible with the Catholic faith."[3] I cannot speak on Church property in some dioceses in the United States because of this. I find all this very painful at times.

But the deeper truth is that my pain often comes from having had unmet expectations of how I should be received or that institutional leaders would talk to me or ask about my views. My prayer led me to see that beneath these expectations were my effort at control and desire to be accepted.

Holding a care for the 100% at the center of my meditation led me to see that the rejection by some institutional leaders forced us into settings where we would not otherwise have gone. Because of not being able to speak on some Catholic properties, we have been catapulted into the interfaith and secular setting. We bring the message of faithful inclusion to people who would not otherwise hear it.

The gift of the Spirit is that the rejection has pushed us into the sea of people who are hungry for spiritual nourishment but often turned off by rigid hierarchical religious structures. The Spirit has pushed us out of our comfort zone of acceptability in order to meet the needs of people we had not known were ours.

In many ways, we are a bit like the senators who close themselves off from the needs of their constituents. We could get caught in the pain of rejection and blame, fighting against an unjust judgment. But for me, the contemplative perspective leads to letting go of my desires and control while opening to the gift of the moment. My consistent learning is that behind the loss is always a surprise, opening into something new. There are prices to be paid, but they are small when compared to the hunger of our people.

Religion/politics is at the heart of my contemplative practice. I am nourished daily by the people I meet and whose stories I hear. My heart is broken open by the truth of their hunger and hope. It is not a theoretical reality for me. Rather, it is the proclamation of the Gospel: Go and preach the good news! The blind see! The lame walk! So my meditation has become breath, that we might see, that we might walk, and, in the process, heal our society that is famished for community and knowing that we belong to each other.

Let us pray together: Come Holy Spirit. Fill the hearts of your faithful and enkindle in us the fire of your love! •

A Spirituality of
Political *Kenosis*

By Eric Martin

After Fr. Dan Berrigan passed away on April 30, 2016, hundreds of people whose lives he touched went marching through the heavy rain from Maryhouse Catholic Worker in Manhattan to The Church of St. Francis Xavier for his funeral Mass. We stopped on the church steps to sing in jubilation, "I'm gonna lay down my sword and shield, down by the riverside, ain't gonna study war no more!" Much was said as half the people in the pews sat dripping on the other half, who drove or took the subway. Most memorable to me was the message from his sister-in-law, Liz McAlister, who had for years organized, witnessed, gone to jail, and prayed with the Jesuit priest-poet. "Sisters and brothers, it is of no service to Dan or to his memory for us to simply hold him up as an icon, especially in ways that exempt us from responsibility," she proclaimed. "How much better would it be if we asked for a double portion of Dan's spirit, and better yet, if we acted on it?"[1]

Understanding what "a double portion of Dan's spirit" means typically starts by turning to May 17, 1968, when he joined eight other Catholics in stuffing Vietnam War draft files in a trash bin and setting them aflame with napalm, reciting the Lord's Prayer over the pyre with his priestly collar visible before the news cameras. The group was known as the Catonsville Nine and became a symbol for the meeting point of the mystical and the political in a moment of heightened cultural violence. For years, he irked both Christians (including several superiors in his Jesuit order), who viewed the role of religion to be more or less confined to personal prayer and church services, and activists working for social justice without the baggage of religion (such as the Weathermen). However, for many, he and those with whom he worked had resurfaced an ancient truth in new garb. Like the prophets of scripture, Berrigan grasped that personal faith cannot be severed from the life of the *polis*, and he decried any attempt by his church to pretend otherwise.

Berrigan was born in 1921. His father's union organizing and his mother's hospitality to those hit hardest by the Depression roused the young boy's political consciousness. Yet, if he had any explicit links to make between his religious vocation and social engagement as a young priest, it was in the precise manner he would later condemn. In 1943, while in the early stages of his Jesuit formation, he wrote to his brother Phil, who was fighting in World War II, that perhaps "our Lord wants you as surely in a field Artillery or Air Force just as surely as he wants fifteen years of study and sweat from me." God, after all, is "Him Who was a good Soldier."[2] Eleven years later, in his final year of formation, he proudly became a military chaplain at Kaiserslautern, America's largest military base outside US soil, where he gave sermons in the shadow of atomic artillery. It was the kind of theological justification and ministerial enablement of patriotic killing that he dedicated the last fifty years of his life to uprooting.

The "Dan Berrigan" remembered in the history books is the result of a long, arduous, and complex conversion. One pivotal moment on this pilgrimage of understanding priestly vocation was a trip to France in 1953–1954. It was there that he met the controversial worker-priests, who had grown out of ecclesial experiments in engaging Marxist laborers who had long been abandoning the church. These

Berrigan grasped that personal faith cannot be severed from the life of the *polis*, and he decried any attempt by his church to pretend otherwise.

priests completely dropped their traditional ministerial duties of preaching in a parish and became, in essence, workers. They went to the factories alongside, worked with, dressed as, lived among, and struggled for unionization with ordinary people. Berrigan was fascinated with this creative presence, so foreign to his training, and felt enlivened by their talks, given in plainclothes to the young novices. He wrote home that he hoped they flourished for the next century: "There are few other signs as hopeful as these in the heavens. Keep them in your prayers."[3]

The pope shut down their ministry only months later, and Berrigan's own superior and retreat master was summoned by Rome for questioning. The example of these priests testing new boundaries, and their official rejection, seems to constitute the first significant challenge to Berrigan's comfortable understanding of both his role as a priest and the church's role in the world. It seemed to him that the worker-priest experiment, as a reaction to Marxism's allure in France, was just the right direction for the church—a way for it to go to the people where they were, rather than a demand for people to come to it. That some of their members had been arrested in a peace protest when an American general came to France must have struck Berrigan as alien, yet it anticipates his later vocation. During his trip to Germany as a military chaplain, however, his maturation was only at its beginning point.

He also traveled around Europe and saw the brutal signs of World War II everywhere, from struggling economies to craters in the earth. In his letters, he noted with admiration the newfound celebrity of Abbé Pierre (1912–2007), who stirred the national consciousness to address rampant homelessness in France. In 1954, when he returned to America to teach high school in New York, he met Dorothy Day (1897–1980) and the Catholic Workers, who had developed a trenchant

Dorothy Day had put into practice the vision of Matthew 25, performing the works of mercy and seeing Christ in those who were hungry, thirsty, in need of food, in prison, or dying.

religious critique of the standing political and economic systems. Though the *Catholic Worker* newspaper was a constant presence in his household growing up, it was through bringing his students to serve at their houses of hospitality during this time that he would meet its co-founder and be changed indelibly by her witness.

He had come at the precise moment that Day and the movement around her were taking a visible political stance against nuclear weapons and war. In 1955, New York began air-raid drills in preparation for a possible Soviet nuclear attack against America. When the signal was given, everyone in the city was to huddle in subway stations and other shelters. Ammon Hennacy (1893–1970), the self-proclaimed "one-man revolution," brought this to Day's attention and suggested resisting. Being no stranger to jail, she immediately agreed. They placed themselves in the park across the street from City Hall and carried leaflets that read, "We do not have faith in God if we depend upon the Atom Bomb." For seven years they protested, and again Berrigan had in front of him a group of people with deep faith, immersing themselves in the political realities of the time, facing arrest for protesting war.

But Day's witness was not limited to public displays and going to jail. Central to the Catholic Worker movement were its houses of hospitality. In New York, they had been taking in the homeless and hungry since 1933 to feed, shelter, and care for them in a direct and human way that no corporate or state bureaucracy ever could. Day had put into practice the vision of Matthew 25, performing the works of mercy and seeing Christ in those who were hungry, thirsty, in need of food, in prison, or dying. It was a form of ministry not at all unlike that of the worker-priests: Forsaking traditional methods to join the neglected where they were and living among them without privilege. Like the worker-priests, Day's deepest religious self could only be expressed in the bi-directional spirituality of divinizing the victims of what she called "this filthy rotten system" by acting upon their humanity and protesting the military, state, and economic apparatus that inevitably dehumanized the least of these.

In the witness of both the worker-priests and the Catholic Worker, Berrigan encountered a discipleship of political *kenosis*. Their approach to social evils was not to devise a more genius system or create a committee to handle problems. Rather, they emptied themselves in prayerful community to directly serve those before them, placing themselves on the same level. They did not call for the overthrow of the government, but for prophetic denunciation, repentance, and conversion. Seeking a "revolution of the heart," as Day called it, they differed from other revolutionaries of the century like Vladimir Lenin (1870–1924) and Fidel Castro (1926–2016). Rather than kill to attain power, they worked to relinquish the little they had–Day emptying herself of a college education and marriage, the worker-priests giving up their traditional ministry and its comforts. They sought

> to be one with [people], to be incarnated in their lives; to be workers with the workers, peasants with the peasants; to share their joys, struggles, troubles, and prayers; to unite contemplation and action by vivifying both; to rediscover the sacred meaning of all things, and make the whole of human life the road which leads to [God].[4]

Berrigan still had a long path to walk from 1961 to Catonsville in 1968. He would march in Selma with Dr. Martin Luther King, Jr., (1929–1968) and attend his famous "I Have A Dream" speech in 1963, travel to South Africa to preach against apartheid with the women of the Grail, go behind the Iron Curtain to discover life under Communist rule, be exiled by his order to Latin America while poor communities were empowering themselves through an emerging theology of liberation, and fly to Hanoi with the historian Howard Zinn (1922–2010) to collect three American prisoners of war and experience life in a bomb shelter under the weaponry of the US military. But it was the example of the worker-priests and Catholic Workers that gave him his footing through it all. He would adopt their spirituality of political *kenosis* in his own way, opting to join those in prison, not as a chaplain or visitor, but as one of them.

As Dorothy Day described with her own conversion, Berrigan took "the downward path to salvation,"[5] becoming a fool for Christ who took upon himself a poverty of freedom as an antidote to the political and economic systems that declared the lives of Vietnamese villagers expendable. His primary resources for half a century were the Beatitudes and Matthew 25, where Jesus self-identifies with the least of these. The worker-priests and Catholic Workers were the first to reveal to him what creative manifestation that might take in the contemporary political milieu.

So, when Liz McAlister proclaimed at Berrigan's funeral that the world needed a "double portion of Dan's spirit," she emphasized that his legacy was not meant to be petrified in an icon. That is certainly not how he saw the worker-priests or Dorothy Day. Rather, he places before us a responsibility to interpret the Gospels with our heads and our hearts–but also our feet and our hands, even if they end up in chains. In the present moment, with its heightened need for spiritual and contemplative attention to political and economic levers, his turn to engaged *kenosis* instead of marshaling power for this or that leader is worthy of attention. It is one way to meet our communal dread with hope.

Luckily, Berrigan left Zen-like blueprints for navigating this downward path in a 1979 interview, when he was asked about plans for the future. "It's no different than the past," he replied. "Opportunity for more growth, and more prayer, and more salvation." But, interjected the interviewer, what about political plans? "That's the political plan," he said. Was he sure? "Absolutely."[6] •

Faith in a Prison Cell:

A Personal Narrative of Transformation

By Peter Armstrong

Y ALARM WENT off at 5:00 a.m. that Tuesday morning in mid-January. I rolled out of bed, drank my coffee, and went quickly into my morning meditation. I had a lot to do before I headed out. When the twenty minutes were up and the chime on my phone rang, I made myself a big breakfast, because I had no idea when my next meal would be. As the sun came up over Washington, DC, I started working on emails that I knew I wouldn't be able to respond to later. Finally, when it was just about time to leave, I took a big black marker and wrote on my left arm a quote from Dr. Martin Luther King, Jr., and on my right arm I wrote my girlfriend's phone number, in case I was allowed a free call. With that, I got on my bike and hit the road.

The night before, about fifty people had gathered in a church in the Capitol Hill district to listen as leaders of faith and people who had personally been affected by the death penalty talked about this cruel practice. SueZann Bosler shared with us how her father, a pastor, had always preached about forgiveness and mercy, up until the day he was killed by a knife-wielding intruder in the church parsonage. SueZann had been there and was also attacked when she came to her father's aid. She listened to her father take his last breaths a few feet away as she lay on the floor with multiple knife wounds, feigning death to save her own life. But her story doesn't end there. After she healed from the physical trauma, SueZann went on to become an advocate of abolishing the death penalty and saved the life of the man who took the life of her father. Listening to her story that night, I felt my heart being moved by the power of her lived example of witness to the Gospel.

After SueZann spoke, we also heard from a man named Derrick Jamison. Derrick is a black man who, along with countless other black people across the country, suffers from a racist system that falsely accuses people of color at a much higher rate than white people.[1] Derrick spent twenty years of his life on death row for a crime he didn't commit, until he was finally exonerated by new evidence and walked free. He stated that the government spent more than eighteen million dollars trying to kill him, but, in the end, failed to do so. Hearing him talk, I could see only the surface of the injustice that he had endured for all those years and knew I would never be able to fully comprehend what he had experienced. Most impressive of all, however, was to hear that, on that day in January, he was preparing to go with us the next morning to the steps of the US Supreme Court, just a few blocks from the church where we had gathered, to engage in civil disobedience against the death penalty. This action would take place on the day before another man, Ricky Gray, was set to be executed in nearby Virginia and it would be Derrick's first time to return to jail since he had been set free.

At the end of the evening, Shane Claiborne gathered us all in prayer, to center us on the stories we had heard that night and take a moment to let all that we had experienced together sink in. Those of us who were willing to engage in civil disobedience the next morning were asked to take a stand and gather in the center for prayer. I stood, moved by the stories I had just heard and still unsure of what I was getting myself into. I felt the weight of what I was signing up for sink in as we received blessings from others who were there to support us. Afterward, those from out of town returned to the Dorothy Day Catholic Worker house, where they were staying, and I went home to my group house in Columbia Heights.

That next day, prepared for the day's protest action, I headed out on my bike. I met the other protesters at the lobbying office of the United Methodist Church, across the street from the Supreme Court. It was a gray, somber day, and it started to rain just as we were walking over to the Supreme Court building to begin our protest. Those of us who had planned to engage in civil disobedience walked up the marble steps and unfurled a banner that stated, "STOP EXECUTIONS!" Meanwhile, more than a hundred additional protesters stood on the sidewalk below. In the pouring rain, the two groups of people–separated by about fifty yards–sang in unison words rooted in the prophet Jeremiah (see 17:8):

> We shall not, we shall not be moved
> We shall not, we shall not be moved
> Just like a tree, that's standing by the water
> We shall not be moved.

Meanwhile, the police officers took us aside, one by one, zip-tied our wrists, and took us away to the Central Detention Facility.

It seemed like a long time before I saw daylight again. We were all put into our cells and I spent the rest of the day and that night lying on my back on a cushion-less steel tray of a bunk bed. I tried not to move around too much, because the steel underneath my back would indent itself and then pop back out again with a loud bang–as if I were lying on the roof of a car. The cockroaches seemed to increase in size and number as the night wore on and a light blazed right above my eyes in the upper bunk. It was a difficult night, and I never did get my one phone call. In the words of faith leader, activist, and author Lisa Sharon Harper, one of the #DC18

The entire Gospel of Luke is one long lesson in speaking truth to power.

who got arrested on that day, "Halfway I wondered if I could make it" out of the "bowels of D.C.'s domestic hell."[2] Luckily, I eventually figured out a way to use one of my boots for a pillow and to block out some of the light by removing one arm from a sleeve and folding it over my eyes so that I could finally get some rest.

During those sixteen hours I lay waiting for something to happen, I had a lot of time to reflect on how I ended up in that little jail cell. This certainly wasn't what I would have predicted when I first became a Christian, just two years prior, during my senior year in college. At that time, I had little or no interest in political engagement and even actively worked to keep the religious student group with which I was involved at Georgetown out of the university's politics. I was interested in faith and Christianity because of the contemplative tradition I was exploring through my own reading and practice of meditation; the idea of a God who works through us in daily life, transforms us through prayer, and ultimately comes to live within and among us is what drew, and still draws, me back to faith. But that faith had very little to do with getting arrested on the steps of the Supreme Court building and fighting to change our country's laws–or so I thought at the time.

Little did I know, back then, that I would soon be nudged in the direction of a deeper engagement with our society's politics, and, ultimately, my own faith. Upon graduating from college, I went to live for a year on the north side of St. Louis, not far from Ferguson, with a program called the Episcopal Service Corps. I had recently joined the Episcopal Church and was talking with my rector about becoming a priest, and she advised me to take a year to engage fully with the Church and see if it really aligned with all that I imagined it to be. I was thrown into the post-Ferguson social justice activist environment of St. Louis, where I quickly began learning about my own white privilege and what I needed to do to help dismantle the oppressive systems from which I benefited. #BlackLivesMatter was on everybody's minds, so I started going to protests, teach-ins, book talks, and other events to learn more, feel more, and get a glimpse of and better understand the gap between the experiences of white and black Americans.

In the end, it was through relationships with people different from myself that I was convinced of the need to step out into the streets. Just as Jesus was moved to ministry by entering into relationship with other people along his path, we too are moved by stories and relationships. For me, it took actually showing up at different events in order to learn about white (and male, and straight, and other forms of) privilege—and meeting people who were experiencing the negative side of this phenomenon—for me to have my heart transformed with compassion and a desire for action. In short, I could read all about redlining, mass incarceration, and the case for reparations, but it wasn't until I actually started showing up at actions with the intention of being transformed through relationship with other people that I began to want to become a better ally.

As a straight white man whose faith has been formed in contemplative Christian circles, places dominated by white, male speakers (even if the majority of audiences consist of women), I need to seek out voices that are different from my own. In a multicultural, multiethnic, pluralistic society, choosing to live comfortably in a bubble of people who share almost everything in common with me—as I have done for most of my life thus far—is a rejection of God's work of Creation, for God didn't create us all the same. We are not meant to live isolationist lives, because God created diversity and it was good (see Genesis 1). And though I often fail to keep my practice of stepping out of my comfort zone as fastidiously as I do my daily meditation, I take comfort in knowing that even Jesus needed to be called out by the Canaanite woman (see Matthew 15:21–28), and learned from her truth in the process.

The work of getting to know others different than ourselves, made so difficult by our society's divisions, is nevertheless the work of following Jesus. I knew I was going to be transformed by following Derrick, SueZann, and the others up the steps of the Supreme Court building. I knew their stories would take time to sink into my heart, but being there with them, sitting with them through court, and staying in touch even after taking action, has continued to challenge me, reminding me of the ways our society needs to change. It keeps the "WWJD?" question–"What would Jesus do?"–right before my eyes.

We know that Jesus wouldn't execute people. That, for many, is a no-brainer.[3] But the real question is whether we know what Jesus would do with the various societal problems facing us today. Many say that their faith is personal and not to be mixed with their politics. But, in my journey over the past two years, I've come to understand that religion has everything to do with politics. Jesus wasn't executed because he went around healing people; he was crucified as the worst kind of criminal because his Gospel message was viewed as dangerous by the ruling class. In fact, the entire Gospel of Luke is one long lesson in speaking truth to power–to the corrupt elite in Jerusalem. If we Christians claim to have anything to do with Jesus, then we must inherently be engaged with the political issues of our time. We need not seek division and further polarization; however, we can continue to engage in tough debate and conversation across dividing lines, expressing our own deeply held convictions and being willing to be changed by our encounter with the other, because that is the way that Jesus engaged with others.

The eighteen of us who were arrested for protesting the death penalty were finally released from jail on Wednesday evening, after thirty-one hours in the belly of the district's judicial system. I was exhausted, worn out, and could hardly think of anything more than how glad I was to finally be able to eat real food again and lie down on a comfy cushion. But, after biking home and grabbing a quick bite to eat, I headed to my church to catch the end of the monthly Taizé service. We sang our songs, and I said a prayer for Ricky Gray, who was scheduled to be executed later that night. As we sat in the silence, I knew that the past two days had changed me. I was transformed; I was healed. But, most of all, I felt that I had come to a fuller understanding of what it means to follow Jesus.   •

Christian Political Engagement:

An Interview with Michael Plekon

By Shirin McArthur

Shirin McArthur: Your most recent book, *Uncommon Prayer: Prayer in Everyday Experience*, speaks about our life of prayer beyond the doors of the church. How is political involvement an uncommon prayer—or not?

Michael Plekon: If one looks at the New Testament, it is hard not to see the reality of politics in the lives of Jesus and those around him. I realize that many "spiritual" people prefer to separate politics from faith. It keeps things neater, happier, without any conflict. But it's not real! It's not honest, either. Think about the coin with the image of Caesar imprinted on it, the constant questions about what can or cannot be done on the Sabbath, the bickering about who is deserving of God's mercy—just the people of Israel or also the marginalized: the Samaritans, Syro-Phoenicians, Romans, and other non-Jews. Rather than trying to edit politics and the rest of everyday life out of our faith, I believe the example and the teachings of Jesus want us to come to terms with our world, as challenging as that may be.

Shirin: When you consider political involvement by faithful Christians, are there particular saints or holy men and women that come to mind from your tradition? How did/do they live out their uncommon prayers?

Michael: We have the example of so many "living icons," persons of faith to orient us. Mother Maria Skobtsova (1891–1945) was an Orthodox Christian nun who hid Jewish people and other targets of the Gestapo in her Paris houses of hospitality. Very important in our American context was the late Archbishop Iakovos (1911–2005), head of the Greek Orthodox Archdiocese. He fearlessly marched with Dr. Martin Luther King, Jr., at Selma and remained a public voice for civil rights, despite death threats from his own community. The litany of witnesses contains many familiar names but even more with little name recognition at all. I think each of us could start identifying, upon reflection, many who are currently alive and working in our neighborhoods right now.

Most of all, I think we have to start taking seriously our own callings to stand up for those in danger and need. The present political situation in the Trump administration has made this both very clear and extremely critical. When distributing groceries at the food bank based in the church we attend, I and my colleagues have to be aware of ICE agents trolling such public locations, both to terrorize and to detain immigrants and refugees, who are now deemed undesirable in our country. Those to whom we look for examples of doing the works of lovingkindness, such as the few I mentioned, show us that we cannot hide from being Christ to others. Their experiences also indicate that we may pay for doing so.

Another strong voice, witness, and example these days is Papa Francesco, the Bishop of Rome. It should surprise no one that his championing of God's mercy, his making mercy the model of how the church should act—whether toward divorced folk or LGBTQ people or refugees, the many who are challenged and the poor—this preaching of the Gospel of mercy has made him a number of opponents, even enemies, among pastors and church leaders, as well as some lay people.

Shirin: You have said that real transformation is not just about standing with those who are targeted and against hateful acts; it will also entail our seeking to build bridges with those with whom we disagree. Where do you see bridge-building happening? What difference does/can faithfulness make in the strength and capacity of the bridge?

Michael: Bridge-building—others would call it communion or fellowship or reconciliation—yes, this is also necessary. Doing the works of lovingkindness, as have Jesus and other persons of faith, cannot take the form of establishing a wall of enmity, dividing us from those who think differently or who do what is harmful to the weak, those in need, the challenged, and the poor. I do think we must rid ourselves of false piety. By this I mean the all-too-easy ways in which some spiritual people blithely claim to be one, even with those opposed to them, while overlooking the actual disagreements and, worse, the toxic behavior of others.

To be specific, I cannot agree with or support the desire to cut millions of Americans from health insurance coverage because expansion of Medicaid and the subsidies provided to purchase coverage are adding to the deficit. The proposed "replacement" to follow repeal of the Affordable Care Act included an enormous tax cut to the wealthiest fraction of the top 1% of Americans. This kind of lawmaking lacks mercy, is unjust, and must be opposed. Likewise, despite claims that only those with serious criminal records are being singled out for deportation, numerous additional non-documented immigrants are, in fact, being detained and deported. Appeals court judges halted the administration's travel bans because they were the enactment of a campaign promise to exclude Muslims from the US, no matter their vetting and status, rather than the foundation for good bridges.

Shirin: What suggestions would you have for those who want to build spiritually strong political bridges?

Michael: Bridges connecting those with whom we disagree must be built with spiritual, living stones. There are basics upon which we can agree, such as our love for God and God's love for us. I have been blessed, gifted, to have lived in three great church traditions—Roman Catholic, Reformation/Lutheran, and Orthodox. Almost a century ago, the greatest Orthodox theologian of the modern era, Fr. Sergius Bulgakov (1871–1944), confessed that, for all our bickering, even our suspicions, fears, and hatred, God had left us still one. It is from this communion with God that we build or, if necessary, rebuild bridges

How will we stay peacemakers as well as resisters unless we practice the works of lovingkindness, forgiving as we are forgiven?

with those who do not share our vision. We have to proceed "as if" there still remains fellowship in the Lord of all. As Martin Luther (1483–1546) said, we must always put the "best construction" on what challenges us.

Shirin: What do you say to those who are tired of division, "us vs. them," and confrontation in the political sphere?

Michael: I say to all of us who are weary—and we *all* are weary: Do not fear, little flock, our Father gave us the kingdom—that is, the beauty and the power of God's presence among us. We are not alone, left to our own devices. In the worst of times in the past, as the lives of so many persons of faith have taught me—over against the terror of the Russian revolution and the Nazi machine of death, in the face of crippling poverty in the Great Depression, during the paralyzing suspicion of the Cold War and then the destructive wars in Vietnam, Iraq, and Afghanistan—women and men continued to hold on to God and not only read the scriptures and prayed, but also did works of mercy for those in need around them. There is always some work of God that I can do. I need to look around me, carefully, to find it.

Shirin: What do you think Jesus would have to say about the political climate in the US over the past decade or so?

Michael: I will just say this, as I did at the start: We cannot try to run from what is ugly and threatening into a spirituality of escape. Likewise, not every one of us is capable of being elected to political office, leading a movement, starting a shelter or food bank or soup kitchen. Jesus would notice where we no longer trust those different from us, and even despise them. Jesus would also call us out for punishing the victims of financial havoc and corporate greed as if they were the perpetrators. There appears, in the current administration, to be an agenda of deconstructing the "administrative state." This is being lauded as a step toward freedom for us, releasing us from any obligation to help others or share with the less fortunate.

Since the start of the last century, some of our best presidents and other government leaders have envisioned God's justice (and I would say mercy) as there being no one left in need of food, clothing, shelter, or medical care. Jesus saw enough of the Roman empire's occupation of Palestine to know the power of military might, the power of the state to tax, to control, to take the lives of those who stood in the way. We cannot be God's children and, at the same time, only want the "hard power" of military might without the mercy of caring for those in need. Thus it seems clear that Jesus would not weep, but rather drive out those who turned his Father's house and world into a marketplace of greed for only the wealthy few because it was assumed that their prosperity would "trickle down" to the rest of us. It simply does not.

Shirin: You say that the new Jerusalem, at the end of times, is when all will truly be "great again"–riffing off President Trump's campaign theme. If Christ's return will usher in this new Jerusalem, why do faithful Christians need to participate in the political arena?

Michael: Oh, but nowhere in the Book of Revelation, nor, for that matter, anywhere else in the New Testament, is the "new Jerusalem" some kind of magical "happy ending" staged by God for those remaining! That book was written to console communities being oppressed, people suffering all kinds of official, but also local, harassment, simply for being who they were. The new Jerusalem, like the "kingdom" of heaven, is an image of when God will be "all in all."

The idea of making America "great again" would be a splendid, godly project if it were the vision of Isaiah, that the lion would lie down with the lamb, that spears would be turned into plows and farming tools, that every suffering and sadness would be taken away–poverty, discrimination, sickness. It is the vision seen by all those hungry people who followed Jesus out into the middle of nowhere, sharing just a couple loaves of bread and dried fish and having an abundance precisely because they trusted and loved enough to share. The miracle in that, and everywhere else in the scriptures, is never a magician doing tricks. Rather, it is always ordinary folks like you and me seeing everything differently, seeing as God sees–and acting upon it.

Shirin: What else would you like to discuss in this intersection of politics and religion?

Michael: I suppose it would be best to close with some concrete things. I would say, in this time—a most challenging one—we need a combination of both resistance and constructive, healing action. It is important, for example, to look around your building or your block and the wider neighborhood. There are specific things you can do: Volunteer at a seniors' or veterans' center, at a soup kitchen or food bank, where there are English classes for immigrants or after-school tutoring for kids. Political divisions should not prevent us from direct assistance to others in need.

As a university professor for over forty years, I believe that staying educated and knowledgeable about what is happening in the country is crucial. All talk of "fake news" and partisan media aside, we need to know the contents of new legislation, and of legislation being repealed. Hearsay and "alternate facts"—that is, non-truths—are destructive. So, too, is retreating, escaping from what is happening, only to then feel frustrated and angry. It is very good to talk to those who are concerned about the administration's direction. It is also important to listen to the "other side," to understand the opposing positions and their reasoning, even if they are objectionable. Only an examined life is a life worth living.

Lastly, we should realize that our spiritual aims and tools of the trade need not be expressed in pious, traditionally "religious" ways. Political and social engagement can be suffused with the spirit of the Gospel. Our actions preach the Gospel. How else will we hear what God has to say unless we put ourselves before God, silently; unless we read the scriptures; unless we lift up our world and those around us in intercession? How will we stay peacemakers as well as resisters unless we practice the works of lovingkindness, forgiving as we are forgiven? To paraphrase Dr. King, we will never extinguish hatred except by love and forgiveness. •

Stone and Star

By Avideh Shashaani

OULD MOSES, JESUS, and Muhammad fight each other if they lived at the same time? If so, what would they fight over? If not, what do we need to understand about what they experienced and taught?

More wars have been waged, and are being waged, in the name of religion than we would like to acknowledge. If we take the three Abrahamic religions—Judaism, Christianity, and Islam—that have the same patriarch and are all monotheistic religions, should we not ask ourselves why they are fighting with such fervor?

Believers of every religion vary in their faith expressions—from the radicals to the mystics—depending on how deeply they experience the essence of what their religion teaches. Each group, let alone each individual, has a different perspective on the religion it practices. So, who really speaks for any religion? Which branch of Judaism, Christianity, or Islam is the "true and authentic" voice of the religion?

Many spiritual traditions have recounted the story of the elephant and the blind men to explain the diversity in our experience of the Divine. Rumi (1207–1273), the Islamic mystic, retold the story in his *Masnavi*. He said some Hindus brought an elephant into a dark room. Depending on where each person touched the elephant, they believed the elephant to be like a water spout (trunk), a fan (ear), a pillar (leg), and a throne (back).[1]

Rumi uses this story to tell us that, if we have the "complete experience" of God, we would not have different explanations or interpretations of God.

Studying deeply the life of the mystics, we see that they arrived at the "fullness" of their faith much like scientists in quest of a discovery. One group searches for God while the other wants to discover the laws of the universe. One's realm of search is the heart/spirit while the other is the world of physical perceptions. Once the discovery is made, there is no dispute. Mystics validate each other's discoveries through the laboratory of the heart and scientists do the same through their respective physical laboratories.

Ibn al-'Arabī (1165–1240), one of the most celebrated Muslim mystics, has said,

> My heart has become capable of every form: it is a pasture
> for gazelles and a convent for Christian monks,
> and a temple for idols and the pilgrim's Ka'ba and the
> tables of the Tora and the book of the Koran.
> I follow the religion of Love: whatever way Love's
> camels take, that is my religion and my faith.[2]

The mystics are driven to discover and experience for themselves what the promulgators of their faiths taught and the way they arrived at their intimate experience of God. If we look at the lives of Moses, Jesus, and Muhammad, we see that they did not arrive at their faith through scholarship or blind acceptance of what their societies taught, but through an urge to "know" the Truth. They spent long periods in spiritual retreats in order to receive inspiration and guidance. Once the guidance came, they gave up everything to serve humanity. We cannot deny their courage in the face of hardships, torments, and afflictions.

If we look with an unbiased lens at the heart of any religion, it is easily seen that they are giving us a manual to discover and be

There is not
one religion that does not
ask us to be charitable, truthful,
just, and compassionate.

in harmony with our "heart/spiritual core"–that which is rooted in universal truths. There is not one religion that does not ask us to be charitable, truthful, just, and compassionate. Why is it, then, that we do not live in a more harmonious and equitable world?

The depth with which we are connected to our heart/spiritual core determines how we respond to situations that demand sacrifice and courage. This direct link to our heart/spiritual core is what I propose to be our conscience–the awareness of universal and unchangeable truths such as justice, integrity, love, and compassion. Rainer Maria Rilke (1875–1926) said, "One moment your life is a stone in you, and the next, a star."[3]

Thus, conscience becomes the trustee and engages in acts that are mutually beneficial and not detrimental to the well-being of others. This is the very foundation of what religion teaches. Those who live the very "heart" of their religion and for whom the edicts of faith are not mere rituals, arrive at and drink from the same river–the river of Oneness. A river may be called by a different name as it passes from one country to another, but it is the same river and has no boundary. A river doesn't call itself by any name or abide by any boundary.

In 2005, the Fund for the Future of our Children launched the Children of Abraham Peace Essay Contest. We asked high school students to reflect deeply about the wisdom found in the Abrahamic traditions and apply that wisdom to an action project.

Year after year, these young people have demonstrated that it is possible to look with an unfiltered lens and an open mind at the underlying principles of these faiths and come away with a unifying and peaceful approach to what "the other" has said.

I am hopeful that young people will lead the way to a more peaceful coexistence. They have not yet developed a "self-interest" perspective in judging "the other" and they understand the fragility of our planet. They do not want to burden it with needless conflicts and alienation. They listen to the voice of their conscience and have the courage to stand up for justice and serve the underserved of our planet.   •

Islam and Politics

By John L. Esposito

ONLY A FEW decades ago, the prevailing wisdom in the West (America and Europe) was that modernization meant the Westernization and secularization of society. This belief was at the heart of modernization and development theories. The West was seen as the model to be emulated by developing countries. As one prominent scholar of the Middle East put it, the choice in the Muslim world was between "Mecca and mechanization."

In recent decades, to the astonishment of many, we have seen a retreat from the secular path, a global resurgence of religion in politics, including the Religious Right in American politics, Christian Liberation Theology in Latin America, and Jewish fundamentalism in Israel. In India, the rise of Hindu nationalism is reflected in the election of the Bharatiya Janata Party (BJP) in an ostensibly secular state and multiple Hindu-Muslim and Hindu-Christian communal conflicts. In Myanmar (formerly Burma), we see a conflict between militant Buddhist monks and the Muslim Rohingya minority.

The intersection of religion and politics enjoys a special place in the history of Middle Eastern Judaism, Christianity, and Islam.

However, in Europe, the experiences of the Renaissance, Enlightenment, and Protestant Reformation were indigenous and precipitated the secularization of politics in the West. Secularism, the separation of religion and politics, came to be accepted as the political development norm by many governments, policymakers, experts, and the media. In contrast to the West's experience, the emphasis on secular values came to the Middle East and broader Muslim world through European colonization. The mingling of religion and traditional forms of governance had never been as discredited as it was in the West. Tradition and religion in the Muslim world, although marginalized, continued to play a role in society and politics. There was no mass intellectual and political movement that explicitly sought to secularize the Middle East.

The prominent reassertion of Islam in Muslim politics, which began in the late 1960s and 1970s, was rooted in a religious revivalism that affected both Muslims' personal and public life. Common to this contemporary religious resurgence is a quest for identity, authenticity, and community, and a desire to establish meaning and order, personally and in society. On the one hand, many became more religiously observant, emphasizing prayer, fasting, dress, and family values. On the other, Islam reemerged as a religio-political alternative to failed nationalist ideologies.

Governments and Islamic movements, both moderate and militant-extremist, used religion to mobilize popular support for their programs and policies. Faith and politics combined to address the problems of political and social injustice (authoritarian governments, repression, maldistribution of wealth, and corruption as well as unemployment, inadequate housing, and poor social services) while also seeking to preserve Muslim religious and cultural identity and values that had been threatened by international Western dominance.

A number of visible crises or failures also proved to be catalytic events. The 1967 Six Day War, in which Israel decisively defeated the combined Arab armies of Egypt, Syria, and Jordan, transformed the liberation of Jerusalem/Palestine into a transnational Islamic issue. Then the Pakistan-Bangladesh civil war of 1971–1972 heralded the failure of Muslim nationalism. The Iranian Revolution of 1978–1979 proved to be a pivotal event with long-term global impact and implications for relations between the Muslim world and the West. Finally, the Palestine-Israel conflict grew in strength during the 1980s and spawned its own Islamist movements, among them HAMAS and Islamic Jihad.

Pervasive themes during the Islamic resurgence focused on the failures of Western models of development and the West's disappointing role as an Arab and Muslim ally, as well as fear of the political, economic, and cultural dominance caused by Westernization. Many blamed the ills of their societies on the excessive influence of and dependence upon the West, especially on the superpowers of America and the former Soviet Union. Efforts to modernize were seen as a process of progressive Westernization, secularization, and increasing globalization. Resentment grew against "neo-colonialism"– exported by the West and imposed by local Western-oriented elites– that powerfully undermined Muslim religious and cultural identity and values.

In the later twentieth century, while most Islamic movements developed in response to domestic conditions, international issues and actors increasingly played important roles in Muslim politics: the Soviet-Afghan War; the Arab-Israeli conflict; sanctions against Saddam Hussein's Iraq; the "liberation" of Bosnia, Kashmir, and Chechnya; and Osama bin Laden and al-Qaeda. In addition, countries like Saudi Arabia, Iran, and Libya, as well as individuals, used their petro-dollars and wealth to extend their influence internationally. They promoted their religious and ideological worldviews and politics by supporting government-Islamization programs as well as Islamist movements, mainstream and extremist.

THE LEADERSHIP OF ISLAMIC MOVEMENTS

ISLAMIC POLITICAL AND social movements proved particularly strong among the younger generation, university graduates and young professionals who were recruited from the mosques and universities. Contrary to popular expectations, the membership of movements, especially in Sunni Islam, has not come from religious faculties and the humanities so much as from the fields of science, engineering, education, law, and medicine. Thus, the senior leadership of many movements includes judges, lawyers, teachers, engineers, physicians, journalists, and prosperous businessmen. At the same time, leaders of militant movements like Egypt's Islamic Jihad, Osama bin Laden's al-Qaeda, and those specifically responsible for the attacks of 9/11 also included many university graduates.

IDEOLOGICAL WORLDVIEW

ISLAMISTS STRESS THAT the Muslim world's state of decline is due to corrupt authoritarian and un-Islamic regimes and excessive political, economic, and cultural dependence on the West. The cure is a return to the faith and values of Islam. Islam, they assert, is a comprehensive ideology or framework for Muslim society that embraces public as well as personal life. They believe that the renewal and revitalization of Muslim governments and societies require the restoration or reimplementation of Islamic law and values, the blueprint for an Islamically guided and socially just state and society. While the Westernization and secularization of society are condemned, modernization, as such, is not. Science and technology are accepted, but the pace, direction, and extent of change must be subordinated to Islamic belief and values in order to guard against excessive influence from and dependence on the West.

THE QUIET REVOLUTION

IN CONTRAST TO the 1980s, when political Islam was simply equated with revolutionary Iran or clandestine groups with names like Islamic Jihad or the Army of God, the Muslim world in the 1990s saw Islamists participating in the electoral process. A quiet revolution had taken place. While a minority of religious extremists sought to impose change from above through terror and holy wars, many others pursued a bottom-up approach, seeking a gradual transformation or Islamization of society through word and example, preaching, and social and political activism.

Islamic organizations and associations emerged as part and parcel of mainstream society, with institutional forces in civil society active in social reform, providing educational, medical, dental, legal, and social-welfare services. Islamic banks and insurance companies as well as publishing houses mushroomed.

This social activism was accompanied by increased political participation. In the late 1980s and 1990s, failed economies and discredited governmental development policies led to political crises and mass demonstrations. These protests resulted in limited political liberalization. Islamic candidates or leaders were elected as mayors and parliamentarians in countries as diverse as Morocco, Egypt, Turkey, Lebanon, Kuwait, Bahrain, Pakistan, Malaysia, and Indonesia. They served in cabinet-level positions and as speakers of national assemblies, prime ministers (in Turkey, Iran, and Pakistan), Deputy Prime Minister (in Malaysia), and Indonesia's first democratically elected president. The general response of many governments to this political power of Islam was to retreat from open elections. They identified their Islamic opposition as extremist and/or simply canceled or manipulated elections, as in Tunisia, Algeria, Egypt, and Jordan.

The majority of Islamists have worked to bring about change through social and political activism within their own societies, by participating, where permitted, in electoral politics and civil society. However, a significant and dangerous minority of extremists, jihad groups from Egypt to Indonesia, al-Qaeda and ISIS, claim a mandate from God to make radical changes since the rulers in the Muslim world and their societies are viewed as anti-Islamic. For these extremists, those individuals and governments who remain apolitical or resist extremist ideas are no longer regarded as Muslims, but rather as atheists or unbelievers, enemies of God, against whom all true Muslims must wage holy war (jihad).

Extremists also believe that Islam and the West are locked in an ongoing battle which stretches back to the early days of Islam, is heavily influenced by the legacy of the Crusades and European colonialism, and is the product today of a Judeo-Christian conspiracy. This conspiracy, they charge, is the result of superpower neo-colonialism and the power of Zionism. The West (Britain, France, and especially the United States) is blamed for its support of un-Islamic or unjust regimes and biased support for Israel in the face of Palestinian occupation and displacement. They portray violence against such governments, their representatives, and citizens (Jews, Christians, and other Muslims, non-combatants as well as combatants) as a legitimate form of self-defense.

OSAMA BIN LADEN AND GLOBAL TERRORISM

S EPTEMBER 11, 2001 was a watershed moment in the history of
political Islam and of the world. Its terror and carnage signalled
the magnitude of the threat posed by Osama bin Laden and
al-Qaeda. The multimillionaire, seemingly devout, university-
educated, wealthy son of a prominent Saudi family had fought against
the Soviets in Afghanistan, a struggle that allied him with a cause
supported by the United States, Saudi Arabia, Pakistan, and many
others. However, after the war, he became radicalized when faced
with the prospect of an American-led coalition in the 1991 Gulf
War to oust Saddam Hussein from his occupation of Kuwait and the
prospect of the presence and increased influence of America in Saudi
Arabia and the Persian Gulf. Osama bin Laden was regarded as the
godfather of global terrorism, a major funder of terrorist groups in
what he claimed was a global jihad.

Osama bin Laden's message appealed to the feelings and grievances of many in the Arab and Muslim world. A critic of American
foreign policy, he denounced its support for Israel, US/UN sanctions
against Iraq that resulted in the deaths of hundreds of thousands of
civilians, and the substantial American (military and economic) presence and involvement in Saudi Arabia that he dismissed as the "new
crusades."

ISIS AND ITS ISLAMIC PEDIGREE AND VISION

L IKE AL-QAEDA, ISIS offers a warped militant Salafi ratio-
nalization to justify, recruit, legitimate, and motivate many of
its fighters. Their unabashed acts of barbarism and terrorism—
slaughter of civilians, savage use of beheadings, killing of innocent
Muslims and Christians—all violate Islamic law.

While there are similarities in ideological worldviews and tactics
between ISIS and other terrorist groups like al-Qaeda, distinctive
differences exist. ISIS has sought to create an Islamic state (a regional
if not global caliphate), to occupy and control areas, to govern, and to
impose their version of a transnational caliphate with its harsh version
of law and order. They are far more ruthless in driving out, suppress-
ing, and executing Shiah Muslims and Kurds, Sunni imams/religious

leaders and others who disagree with them, and they demand conversion to their warped and extraordinarily violent brand of Islam from minorities such as Christians and Yazidis, forcing populations to publicly pledge their allegiance to the caliphate in exchange for security, in a mafia-like version of "protection" and social services.

IS RELIGION THE PRIMARY DRIVER OF THE SO-CALLED ISLAMIC CALIPHATE?

L IKE AL-QAEDA AND others, ISIS's appeal to a harsh and barbaric version of religion/Islam captures headlines. Religion, as well as other factors, do play a role to legitimate, recruit, and motivate followers. However, studies of jihadist movements like ISIS show that the primary motivations are most often political: a declared outrage at the occupation and oppression of Muslims and Muslim lands. Thus, for example, ISIS execution videos reveal the primacy of political grievances: foreign military invasion and occupation and the killing of tens of thousands of civilians, as well the "crimes" committed by individuals or groups (Iraqi soldiers, police, and government workers).

Terrorists like Bin Laden and Abu Bakr al-Baghdadi of ISIS moved beyond classical Islam's criteria for a just *jihad* and recognize no limits but their own. Islam's norms and values about good governance, social justice, and the requirement to defend Islam when under siege were transformed into a call to arms in order to legitimate the use of violence, warfare, and terrorism. Their theology of hate sees the modern world in mutually exclusive, black-and-white categories: the world of belief and unbelief, the land of Islam and of warfare, the forces of good against the forces of evil. Those who are not with them, whether Muslim or non-Muslims, are the enemy and are to be fought and destroyed in a war with no limits, no proportionality of goal or means.

Adopting the worldview of an Islam under siege, they ignore or reject Islamic law's regulations regarding the goals and means of a valid *jihad*: that violence must be proportional, that only the necessary amount of force should be used to repel the enemy, that innocent civilians must be protected, and that *jihad* must be declared by the ruler or head of state. As scholars of the Islamic Research Council at al-Azhar University, regarded by many as the highest moral authority in Islam, forcefully stated in condemning Bin Laden's calls for *jihad* and terrorism:

> Islam provides clear rules and ethical norms that forbid the killing of non-combatants, as well as women, children, and the elderly, and also forbids the pursuit of the enemy in defeat, the execution of those who surrender, the infliction of harm on prisoners of war, and the destruction of property that is not being used in the hostilities.[1]

POLITICAL ISLAM AND THE DEMOCRACY DEBATE

IN RECENT YEARS, the call for greater political participation and democratization has become widespread in many countries in the Muslim world. Diverse sectors of society—secular and religious, leftist and rightist, educated and uneducated—have increasingly used democratization as the litmus test by which to judge the legitimacy of authoritarian, repressive, and corrupt governments. However, most experts and citizens in Muslim countries do not expect significant reform any time soon. Rulers like Egypt's Hosni Mubarak, Tunisia's Zine El Abidine Ben Ali, and Libya's Muammar Qaddafi remained in power for several decades. Hereditary monarchies in Saudi Arabia, the United Arab Emirates, and Jordan are deeply entrenched. All have relied on their militaries, police, and security forces for their rule and protection.

The "Arab Uprisings" or "Arab Spring" in 2011 marked a potentially historic transition in the political makeup of many Muslim countries: Tunisia, Egypt, Libya, Syria, and Bahrain. A broad sector of society—eager for change and democratic reforms—made its voice heard, rebelling against decades-long authoritarian rule, reclaiming its dignity and national pride, and insisting that it would decide the direction and the future of its countries. In Egypt and Tunisia, Islamist candidates and parties, Egypt's Muslim Brotherhood and Tunisia's Ennahda (Renaissance Party), although initially not among the leadership, swept into power in post-uprising democratic elections. New governments faced formidable challenges: to satisfy the multiple needs of diverse sectors of society and, in particular, to jump-start failed economies and address issues of high unemployment and increased expectations. By 2013, the Arab Spring began to look like an Arab winter.

Today, Libya and Syria remain deeply divided. Since 2011, more than two hundred thousand Syrians have been killed, five million have fled to other nations as refugees, and more than six million have been displaced within the country. The governments of both Egypt and Tunisia struggled to govern and to deal with opposition critics and movements. While Tunisia's Rachid Ghannouchi and his Ennahda Party lost the second round of presidential elections, they remain major political players. The hardest hit was Egypt and its first democratically elected President, Mohamed Morsi, an American-trained engineer and member of the Muslim Brotherhood. A nationwide anti-Morsi and anti-Brotherhood protest movement erupted on June 30, 2013, around the anniversary of Morsi's troubled first year in power. Many demanded that Morsi resign or be driven from office. This provided the excuse for a military-backed coup, led by Egyptian army chief General Abdel Fattah el-Sisi, with strong financial support from Saudi Arabia and the United Arab Emirates (UAE), which has resulted in the worst governmental repression and violence in modern Egyptian history. Egypt has returned to authoritarianism, repression, mass arrests, and military trials, drawing sharp criticism and condemnation from major international human rights organizations.　•

A Different Drum

By angel Kyodo williams

Excerpted from *Radical Dharma: Talking Race, Love, and Liberation*

EVERYTHING BEGINS BY LEAVING

PEOPLE ALWAYS ASK about beginnings. We strive after newness, the shiny, the acquisition of possibility. A proxy for our own longing to begin anew on the journey of finding ourselves because we haven't yet gotten there. What we don't often ask is, "What made me choose me?" and "What had to end?" and "What got left behind?"

STAGES AND VOWS

PERHAPS IT HAD just come out, I don't remember any longer, but the bright yellow cover of M. Scott Peck's book *The Different Drum* caught my eye's attention, though it was its title that caught my soul. I had always been a different drum, even when

I looked the same. Most of my early life was spent desperately wanting to be the same, trying to fit the molds handed to me and the ones I thought I belonged in, only to realize with stunning certainty that I, in fact, did not. Rinse. Wash. Repeat.

Peck's proposed stages eventually provided a lens through which I continue to envision the spiritual and the political life journeys as simultaneously parallel and intertwined. More acutely, Peck's stages gave me the answer to a question I'd held in stubborn arrogance, one that prevented me from seeing people who counted themselves part of some religion–most especially Christianity– with respect. By that time, I had developed growing admiration for obvious figures like Desmond Tutu, His Holiness the Dalai Lama, but also Malcolm X and the great Dalit hero and liberator of the Untouchables, Bhimrao Ambedkar. They were, by all appearances, religious. But they seemed smart, reasonable, and deeply concerned with social justice, too. Not only did Peck's description of development unseat the stubborn aversion I had to other people's religiosity, it also freed me to accept my own path as not just philosophical but spiritual, too....Turns out that the Four Vows, written for ordinary lay folk as far back as 1,500 years ago, and uttered at the end of every Zen practice session, speak to each of Peck's stages. I take these vows again and again, marking my life's journey through these stages as practice....

STAGE I: CHAOS–EARLY CHILDHOOD:
TOLD WHERE TO GO, WILLED AND CONTROLLED

Beings are numberless; I vow to save them all.

LIKE MANY CHILDREN born "into" a religion or tradition, Christianity by way of the Black Baptist Church wasn't a choice I was given so much as a place I was made to go. I was toted along like a shiny Sunday handbag. It meant having my hair pulled and twisted into pristine "Shirley Temple curls," spotless white patent leather shoes with pom-pom socks sitting just so beneath unscuffed caramel brown knees, dresses of just enough delicate white lace and frills so that there was never a safe place to sit, and a paper doily pinned uncomfortably to my head.

My earliest recollection of a life utterly controlled by an abusive babysitter-turned-pseudo-mom was the weekly pomp and circumstance of going to church. It is also the most poignant reminder of the gross conflict between the life we lived in full view of everyone and the one that went down behind closed doors where the yelling, shaming, emotional manipulation, arm-twisting, head-thrust-into-the-flushing-toilet scenes were performed alongside the rehearsal of stories that obscured the truth.

My father was raised Catholic. D took care of me from soon after my mother left to spare herself my father's philandering. He was a firefighter by night and day, and a womanizer in the spaces between. It was the early '70s—love was free and boys will be boys, after all. D was seventeen when she came into my life…red-bone bright with gleaming hazel eyes and a big, welcoming smile. No one would suspect she was a faithful product of the good and pious church lady's den of abuse and molestation that was held together by fear.

It was D's church I first recall. I liked the choir, so I tried to make it work, but it never really did—the other big church ladies fanning, folks faintin' and hollerin' as they caught the Holy Ghost streaking down the aisles. The pretense of Sunday-only proper manners in other peoples' company mixed with stylized high drama fit for its own reality show and threw into relief the falsehood of my own overwhelming existence.

My role was to submit to the highest and most fearful authority, and I did as I was willed. My lighter skin and springy "good hair" that could be tightly controlled made me the best kind of windup doll. A child model who was a model child: starting school early but still commanding the three Rs better than anyone, being brilliant in every way as if by shining so bright no one would really see me and the suffering I endured.

I was toted along like a shiny Sunday handbag.

STAGE II: FORMAL–ADHERENCE TO ORDER AND RULES

Desires are inexhaustible; I vow to put an end to them.

B Y THE TIME I was eight, D's sadistic ways had been found out. Both the harrowed life and only motherly love I could remember disappeared overnight.

My father's relationship with his newest girlfriend was serious enough to take us to Brooklyn. It was the heart of Flatbush and the height of the West Indian population explosion there. I was a foreigner in my own homeland, navigating a sea of Black faces that I felt neither kin nor camaraderie with. The golden years of living in the wildly multicultural Lefrak City–a kind of United Nations of massive housing in Queens–were now behind me. The safety of being different among difference was left against my will....

Many of the West Indians despised us Yankees for our mis-storied laziness, and yet envied the security of citizenship; we were all caught in the territorial wars waged between Black bodies vying for a higher place on the lowest rung of the totem pole reserved for us in the land of the freely white. The Hasidic Jews and Italians eventually receded to the higher ground that white-skinned people always seem to find when a tide of Black and brown rolls in. Rather than seeing ourselves as aligned, we were repositioned as bottom-feeders fighting among ourselves for the rotting remnants and decay white folks left behind....

My stepmother had an enormous white King James-version of the Bible gilded in gold. Along with the twenty-one-book set of brown and black World Book Encyclopedias and Childcraft books she sold and I immersed myself in, that Bible became yet another hiding place for me.... My new stepmother's Episcopalian church was a welcome relief from the ecstatic drama of D's church. I took refuge not so much in the church but in the silence I found.

While I was always skeptical, the stories were entertaining enough, so I perused the Bible. Dissecting the scenarios provided hours of fodder for my imagination: the greatest refuge of the shy, introverted, non-belonging. I secretly wanted to be a priest but was already a "tomboy" and knew women in the church and military had to wear dresses, which wasn't happening now that I had a say.

Me and Jesus were getting along fine. I knew things didn't turn out for the best for Christ given the images of the emaciated and wounded white man with pained blue eyes I'd grown up with, but I wasn't prepared for confronting his agony.

> About the ninth hour, Jesus cried out with a loud voice, saying, "Eli, eli, lama sabachthani"–My God, my God, why hast thou forsaken me? –Matthew 27:45–46

I was angry. How could God forsake him? What kind of good could this God ever be if so cruel? He'd turned his back while his only child suffered alone and in the dark. For some time, I imagined my anger was because I couldn't make sense of it, but really, I couldn't make sense of how I had been left to bear a burden so great so young because the people in my life–my own father, too–had forsaken me.

STAGE III: DOUBT–SKEPTICISM, REJECTION OF RULES AS GIVEN, INDIVIDUAL INVESTIGATION

The truth is boundless; I vow to perceive it.

BY AGE TWELVE, I'd excused myself from Sunday school, church, and eventually Christianity. School provided me with science as a less painful story of human existence, and my time devouring World Book Encyclopedias gave me access to agnosticism....

'Tweens and Twenties

Mercifully, I escaped Brooklyn and went to live with my mother in lower Manhattan, though I straddled the Brooklyn Bridge and the vastly different worlds it joined together more often than not. The harshness and violence of Flatbush was tempered by the Bohemian understated class of Tribeca. Both of them were set against the backdrop of a Chinatown school that was more than mostly ethnic Chinese, so I lived again as a foreigner in a familiar land. I learned that context was everything, dictating norms of culture, speech, expression of gender, intelligence, and the rules for

I turned and walked away,
leaving my friends behind.

how to belong. This bridging, as both survival function and choice-ful act, taught me a basic Truth: Each world you inhabit is no more or less real than the others. It is all just a protocol, a made-up and agreed-upon set of codes. In fact, moving fluidly between worlds of difference meant developing an awareness of what of "so-called you" remained still and apparently the same.

In my high school years, I explored the wide-open land of no real parental oversight. Cutting school. Lounging in the upscale diner in Chelsea learning the cheeky talk and refinement of every-thing from gay white men. They came in stronger and stronger waves, with their dinner parties, studs, and leather boys, washing over the mostly Puerto Rican and Black families that lived there until those families were drowning and almost none.

Rolling up lesbian, then gay, then mixed clubs through the night, I reveled in the last deep breaths of queer culture in the West Village in the '80s. We didn't know it was dying then because *we* felt most alive.... A natural aversion to the disorderliness of drugs and my high-minded downtown disgust with the sloppiness of being drunk kept me relatively safe in those days....

In the meantime—maybe in response?—gender was becoming more complex. You were no longer policed into a strictly female or male role-play inside of being Lesbian or Gay. BT and eventually Q were finding their way into our landscape and language. We were finding new allies, paving new intersections, telling new stories and seeding a Queer Nation by reclaiming what was meant to shame us. It felt radical and emergent. I was alive and fighting for justice. And then I had to leave.

A trip to San Francisco landed me on a cushion in the tem-ple made famous in my mind by reading Shunryu Suzuki Roshi's book *Zen Mind, Beginner's Mind*. I'd found it by accident rummaging through New York's old Tower Books. The chance to try out medi-tation beyond my closeted setup at home was too much to pass up, even if I had to make my way through an unknown city, already farther away from home than I'd ever been. More than leaving home and my sleeping lover, I'd begun to leave my former self in the still shadowy dawn light that September morning....

Not too much longer after, I knowingly carried my tender grief to the funeral of my relationship with my now grown-up friends. The truth I was seeking was more and more at odds with the stories we told ourselves to be right, to keep fear and overwhelming at bay. Standing increasingly on the outside and no longer wanting to be in, I turned and walked away, leaving my friends behind.

STAGE IV: MYSTIC/COMMUNAL

Liberation is unattainable; I vow to attain it.

THE INTERSECTION AND influencers of my life left little room for some outside and some in....

Being in the territory doesn't make you belong. Every time I tried to stay within the lines, they ran over me, so I chose the borderlands and left divisions behind.

The hero and liar that nurtured me. The mother-punisher who stole from me and stole for me, raised me up and shoved me down. The church lady dealing sin dressed as saint, building a house of protection and pain. The fierce queens from the runways who sex-danced their way to early deaths and lived forever on screen. The Black and brown boys gone to prison, queer colored girls behind bars and behind sassiness that reminded me where I might have been.... The low-key, high-brown urban Bohemians who showed me How to Sit with the invisible cloak of class on, a formless field of benefaction, to exude the quiet cool my Zen would one day be.

Whenever I feel around for me, I find all of them and someone else I didn't know was there before. I want for their liberation because, inside theirs, I found mine. The dharma that I would come to taught me everything I already knew about life—that it is indeed suffering, and the path of liberation is paved with pain and joy but always near when you know you're just looking to return to you and have to leave the home of Me behind.

Enter here. It's everywhere and in everyone.   •

Boundaries

You say,
your God is better than mine.

You say,
your God is mightier than mine.

You say,
your God is loving, kind, forgiving.

I say,
no one has a monopoly on God,
If God is God.

–Avideh Shashaani[1]

NOTES

From Mysticism to Politics

1 Charles Péguy, *Notre Jeunesse*, 1909. https://en.wikipedia.org/wiki/
Charles_P%C3%A9guy#Famous_quotations.

2 For a good overview of the life and contribution of Charles Péguy, see
Robert Royal, "The Mystery of the Passion of Charles Peguy," Catholic
Education Resource Center, found at http://www.catholiceducation.
org/en/culture/art/the-mystery-of-the-passion-of-charles-peguy.html.

3 Of numerous works written in the last thirty years, exploring the
political, social, and economic implications of Jesus' life and teaching, one
which remains a hallmark and is radically changing my thinking is John
Howard Yoder's *The Politics of Jesus* (Grand Rapids: Eerdmans, 1972). A
revised and expanded version was published by Eerdmans in 1994.

4 Edwin H. Friedman, *Generation to Generation: Family Process in Church and
Synagogue* (New York: Guildford Press, 1985).

Confessions of a Preacher in the Borderlands

1 Adolf Hitler, "The Obersalzberg Speech," August 22, 1939. https://
en.wikipedia.org/wiki/Hitler%27s_Obersalzberg_Speech.

2 https://www.azleg.gov/legtext/49leg/2r/bills/sb1070s.pdf.

3 http://cardinalrogermahonyblogsla.blogspot.com/2010/04/arizonas-
new-anti-immigrant-law.html.

4 https://www.youtube.com/watch?v=cbKQudtWqxk.

5 Office of the General Assembly, *Book of Order 2015–2017: The Constitution
of the Presbyterian Church (USA) Part II* (Louisville, KY: The Office of the
General Assembly, 2015), 5.

6 Office of Theology and Worship, *Book of Occasional Services* (Louisville,
KY: Geneva Press, 1999), 24. http://www.pghpresbytery.org/forms/
pdfs/com/Book-of-Occasional-Services.pdf.

7 Walter Brueggemann, "Biblical Authority: A Personal Reflection"

(address to the 2000 Covenant Network of Presbyterians Conference, Pittsburgh, PA, November 3, 2000. http://covnetpres.org/2000/11/biblical-authority-a-personal-reflection/.

A Moment for Something More Soulful Than Politics

1 Scott Neuman, "Trump Lashes Out At McCain: 'I Like People Who Weren't Captured,'" NPR.org, July 18, 2015. http://www.npr.org/sections/thetwo-way/2015/07/18/424169549/trump-lashes-out-at-mccain-i-like-people-who-werent-captured.

2 Mark Twain, "The Czar's Soliloquy," The North American Review, no. DLXXX (March, 1905): 324.

3 Shakespeare, Hamlet, Act 3, Scene 1, 3. http://nfs.sparknotes.com/hamlet/page_138.html.

4 Martin Luther King, Jr., "Address at the Religious Leaders Conference on 11 May 1959," The Papers of Martin Luther King, Jr. (Berkeley: University of California, 2005), 5:200.

A Meditation on Hope and Fear

1 Abraham Joshua Heschel, The Insecurity of Freedom (New York: Farrar, Straus and Giroux, 1967), 4.

2 Thomas Merton, New Seeds of Contemplation (New York: New Directions, 1972), 116.

3 Jürgen Moltmann, The Source of Life (Minneapolis: Fortress Press, 1997), 39.

4 Anthony Kelly, Eschatology and Hope (Maryknoll: Orbis Books, 2006), 201.

5 Ibid., 72.

6 Moltmann, The Source of Life, 39.

7 Krista Tippett, Becoming Wise (New York: Penguin Books, 2016), 233.

8 Kelly, Eschatology and Hope, 6.

9 Jürgen Moltmann, Theology of Hope (Minneapolis: Fortress Press, 1993), 25.

10 Abraham Joshua Heschel, Israel (New York: Farrar, Straus and Giroux, 1974), 94.

11 Kelly, Eschatology and Hope, 57.

12 Josef Pieper, Faith, Hope, Love (San Francisco: Ignatius, 1997), 91.

13 Heschel, Israel, 93.

14 Pieper, *Faith, Hope, Love*, 93.

15 Seneca, *Letters from a Stoic* (London: Penguin Books, 1969), 38.

16 Ernst Bloch, *The Principle of Hope* (Cambridge: MIT Press, 1986), 1:3.

17 Gustavo Gutierrez, *A Theology of Liberation* (Maryknoll: Orbis, 1973), 218.

18 Kelly, *Eschatology and Hope*, 212.

19 Thomas Merton, *No Man Is an Island* (San Diego: Harcourt, 1983), 15.

20 Reinhold Niebuhr, *The Irony of American History* (New York: Scribner, 1952), 63.

21 Kelly, *Eschatology and Hope*, 219.

Knowing the Love of God:
Catherine of Siena's Interior Politics of Tranquility

1 Catherine visited and wrote to Pope Gregory XI toward the end of the "Babylonian Captivity of the Papacy" (1309–1377) and her persuasion was integral to his decision to return the papacy to Rome.

2 Catherine of Siena, *The Dialogue*, trans. Suzanne Noffke (Mahwah, NJ: Paulist Press, 1980), 50.

3 Giacinto D'Urso, OP, *Catherine of Siena, Doctor of the Church: Notes on Her Life and Teaching*, trans. Thomas McDermott, OP (Chicago: New Priory Press, 2013), 12.

4 Paul Ricœur, *Oneself as Another*, trans. Kathleen Blamey (Chicago: University of Chicago Press, 1992), 2.

5 Ibid., 116–117.

6 Ibid., 117.

7 Ricœur, *Oneself as Another*, 118; it is unclear whether, for Ricœur, the identity characterized by perseverance through time remains wholly unknown, in the sense of the Kantian "thing in itself." It is at least clear that, for Catherine, this self is indeed unknown, but that it also does not remain that way.

8 D'Urso, *Catherine of Siena*, 12.

9 Bernard McGinn, *The Varieties of Vernacular Mysticism: 1350–1550* (New York: Crossroad, 2012), 235.

10 *Dialogue*, 40.

11 D'Urso, *Catherine of Siena*, 13.

12 *Dialogue*, 48.

13 Ibid., 27.

14 Ibid., 36.

15 Ricœur, *Oneself as Another*, 2–3.

16 Ibid., 113.

17 Ibid., 122.

18 McGinn, *Varieties of Vernacular Mysticism*, 223.

19 *Dialogue*, 27.

20 Ibid., 73.

21 Ibid.

22 Ibid., 82.

23 Ibid., 25.

24 Ibid., 40.

25 Ibid., 42.

26 McGinn, *Varieties of Vernacular Mysticism*, 236.

27 *Dialogue*, 25.

28 Ibid., 33.

29 D'Urso, *Catherine of Siena*, 13.

30 Ibid., 14.

31 *Dialogue*, 33.

32 Ibid., 27.

33 Ibid., 26.

34 Ibid., 153.

35 McGinn, *Varieties of Vernacular Mysticism*, 221.

36 *Dialogue*, 29.

37 Ibid., 49.

38 Ibid., 37.

Religion and Politics

1 Pope Francis, *Evangelii Gaudium* (Washington, DC: United States Conference of Catholic Bishops, 2014), paragraph 204.

2 Cindy Wooden, "Health care is a right, not a privilege, pope says," *Catholic News Service*, May 9, 2016. http://www.catholicnews.com/services/englishnews/2016/health-care-is-a-right-not-a-privilege-pope-says.cfm.

3 Public Radio International, "American nuns reprimanded by Vatican for 'radical feminist views,'" PRI, May 2, 2012. https://www.pri.org/stories/2012-05-02/american-nuns-reprimanded-vatican-radical-feminist-views.

A Spirituality of Political Kenosis

1 Beth Griffin, "Father Berrigan hailed as visionary who was ruled by faith at funeral Mass," *America* (May 6, 2016), https://www. americamagazine.org/issue/dan-berrigan-hailed-visionary-ruled-faith.

2 Daniel and Philip Berrigan, *The Berrigan Letters: Personal Correspondence Between Daniel and Philip Berrigan*, ed. Daniel Cosacchi and Eric Martin (Maryknoll, NY: Orbis, 2016), 7.

3 Berrigan and Berrigan, *The Berrigan Letters*, 11.

4 Jean Marie Domenach and Robert de Montvalon, *The Catholic Avant-Garde: French Catholicism Since World War II* (New York: Holt, Rinehart, & Winston, 1967), 58.

5 James T. Fisher, *The Catholic Counterculture in America, 1933–1962* (Chapel Hill, NC: University of North Carolina Press, 1989), 14. She borrowed the phrase from Charles Baudelaire.

6 Daniel Berrigan, "Connecting the Altar to the Pentagon," *Peace is the Way: Writings on Nonviolence from the Fellowship of Reconciliation*, ed. Walter Wink (Maryknoll, NY: Orbis, 2000), 97.

Faith in a Prison Cell: A Personal Narrative of Transformation

1 Rebecca Hersher, "Black People Are Wrongly Convicted Of Murder More Often, Data Show," *NPR.org*, March 7, 2017. http://www.npr. org/sections/thetwo-way/2017/03/07/519012758/black-people-are-wrongly-convicted-of-murder-more-often-data-shows.

2 Lisa Sharon Harper, "One Breath at a Time: 16 Hours in a D.C. Jail," *Sojourners* (January 26, 2017), https://sojo.net/articles/one-breath-time-16-hours-dc-jail.

3 Jonathan Merritt, "Would Jesus Support the Death Penalty?" *TheAtlantic.com*, May 2, 2014. https://www.theatlantic.com/politics/ archive/2014/05/jesus-death-penalty/361649/.

Stone and Star

1 Jalal al-Din Rumi, *Tales from Masnavi*, trans. A.J. Arberry (New York: Routledge, 1993), http://www.khamush.com/tales_from_masnavi. htm#The Elephant.

2 Ibn al-'Arabī, *The Tarjuman al-Ashwaq*, trans. Reynold A. Nicholson, http://www.sacred-texts.com/isl/taa/taa14.htm.

3 "Sunset," *Selected Poems of Rainer Maria Rilke* (New York: Harper, 1981), http://www.yourdailypoem.com/listpoem.jsp?poem_id=20.

Islam and Politics

1 Islamic Research Council, reported in *Al-Hayat*, November 5, 2001, as cited in John L. Esposito, "Struggle in Islam," Boston Review (February/March 2002), http://bostonreview.net/archives/BR27.1/esposito.html#2.

Boundaries

1 Avideh Shashaani, "Boundaries," *Tell Me Where To Be Born* (Annapolis: The Bunny and Crocodile Press, 2008), 52.

Center for
Action and
Contemplation

A collision of opposites forms the cross of Christ.
One leads downward preferring the truth of the humble.
The other moves leftward against the grain.
But all are wrapped safely inside a hidden harmony:
One world, God's cosmos, a benevolent universe.